Escalating Disputes

A PROFMEX Monograph

This study of contemporary changes in law in the villages of the Villa Alta region of Oaxaca, Mexico, focuses on disputing and its relationship to evolving political and religious forces in the region and the larger society. Because the social composition of a peasant village influences the way villagers perceive the order of their larger social universe and the way they participate in it, village legal systems grow and centralize in relation to local stratification and information exchange.

Disputing is an important component of the daily lives of Villaltecos. Through disputes they communicate their views, check up on one another, express their anger, and relieve the tensions bred in village conflicts. As the disputes of Villa Alta escalate beyond the dyadic relationships of neighbors, friends, and close kin to include a broader range of participants from the village, the region, and the city, they grow to encompass some of the major controversies and issues Mexico is facing today. While this provides villagers with the processes and symbols through which they can phrase those issues in relation to local concerns, escalating disputes can also generate new elements of uncertainty as well as social arenas for innovation. This book explores how villagers choose the arena in which they settle their disputes and how these disputes are used to reorder old social formations and to create new ones.

Philip C. Parnell

Escalating Disputes

SOCIAL PARTICIPATION
AND CHANGE
IN THE OAXACAN HIGHLANDS

The University of Arizona Press
Tucson

THE UNIVERSITY OF ARIZONA PRESS
Copyright 1988
The Arizona Board of Regents
All Rights Reserved

Manufactured in the U.S.A.
This book was set in 10/12 Baskerville.

Library of Congress Cataloging-in-Publication Data

Parnell, Philip C.
Escalating disputes : social participation and change in the
Oaxacan highlands / Philip C. Parnell.
p. cm. — (Profmex monograph series)
Bibliography: p.
Includes index.
ISBN 0-8165-1053-9 (alk. paper)
1. Justice, Administration of—Mexico—Oaxaca. 2. Dispute
resolution (Law)—Mexico—Oaxaca. 3. Courts—Mexico—Oaxaca.
4. Oaxaca (Mexico)—Social conditions. I. Title. II. Series.
KGF8130.P37 1988
347.72′7409—dc19
[347.274079]   88-17114
                                                     CIP

British Library Cataloguing in Publication data are available.

To my parents,
Dorothy and Bill Parnell

CONTENTS

ACKNOWLEDGMENTS

I owe a special thanks to Laura Nader who helped clear the paths that led me to the villages of Villa Alta, the state court in the district seat, and the eventual completion of this work. I have found her research and teaching both invigorating and challenging. Villagers in the regions of Villa Alta and Talea share respect and affection for "Laura." Certainly Nader's long-lasting warm relations with the villagers of Oaxaca helped ease my initial acceptance into village life. I have also benefited from Nader's comments on a draft of this work. I owe a special debt of gratitude to Elizabeth Colson who offered instructive comments on two drafts. Her knowledgeable, thoughtful, and insightful comments in our discussions and correspondence have provided me with both support and inspiration.

I am most grateful to the villagers of Villa Alta, especially those of the district seat, Taguí, Lachirioag, and Talea. The government of the district seat Villa Alta wisely required that I, like all residents, contribute my time to the maintenance of the community. My frequent participation in village committees and work groups led to many ties of reciprocity, good companionship, and, even in the midst of some heated disputes, a lot of fun. The residents of the district seat of Villa Alta are not known for their hospitality, yet they eventually opened their homes to me. As I earned the rights of a citizen they voluntarily cared for my welfare. When I returned to Villa Alta for my second period of research in 1984, I was a member of a maturing generation who shared with me their hopes and concerns for the future. Since I have changed all names to guard the privacy of villagers, I cannot here express directly the special thanks I owe to the families with whom I lived and my many other teachers within the region. I hope that this work captures, in its limited ways, some of the challenges, rewards, and social wisdom of villagers in the land of the mountain Zapotec.

The Center for the Study of Law and Society of the University of California at Berkeley, under the direction of Jerome Skolnick, funded my initial research in Villa Alta through a National Institute of Mental

Health Traineeship. A Research Service Award from the United States Public Health Service funded the write-up of that research. My second period of research in Villa Alta, on which this book is primarily based, was funded in part by Indiana University.

Ingeniero Anwar Abdullah of Oaxaca provided me with assistance during my initial research in Villa Alta. My colleague, the historian Ellen Dwyer, was generous with her time and comments in reading the first draft of this work. Two other colleagues, the historian Barbara Hanawalt and the psychologist Cathy Widom, commented on portions of that draft. June Starr and the lawyer Bryant Garth also provided helpful comments and suggestions. I especially want to thank Ken Goodall who helped me place the commas and periods, and Judy Kelley who received and cared for my field notes and let me know each month that they had arrived.

This book is dedicated to my parents, who have always been generous with their love, support, and encouragement.

Escalating Disputes

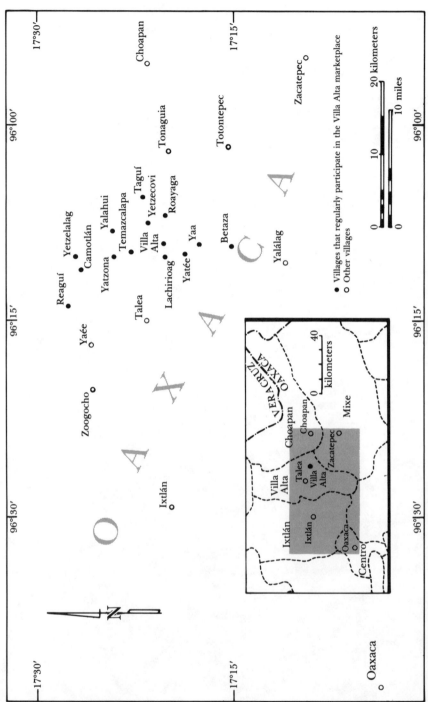

The Villa Alta marketplace region, important relations, and (inset) the district Villa Alta and neighboring districts

CHAPTER 1

Introduction: A Marketplace Region

Law and societies change in many ways. Those who hold positions of judgment and the rationales they use to explain their decisions change as the forces of political revolution, technological invention, religious revitalization, economic development and decline, and violent conquest occupy and reform institutions of societal control. The forces of change may also be as subtle as the accumulation of spoken words, the recognition of grievances, and the interweaving of identities over centuries of social commerce. The construction of social change ultimately is a human endeavor and therefore inexact. The nature of change is as varying as those who create it. Nevertheless, social and legal change achieves both form and quality as those who experience it attempt to assess and define both what they share and how they differ.

This study of the contemporary vicissitudes of law in a region of Mexican villages focuses on disputing and its relationship to evolving political and religious forces in the region and the larger society. My thesis, backed by case histories, is that the social composition of a peasant village influences the way villagers perceive and order their larger social universe and the way they participate in it. Accordingly, village legal systems grow and centralize in relation to local stratification and information exchange. Faced with perceived political and religious threats to village cohesion, a culturally plural and economically stratified village centralizes internally, while more homogeneous villages centralize externally—with disputing as the oil in the process.[1]

The villages of the Villa Alta judicial district, ranging in population from 300 to 4,000, lie along the peaks of the Sierra de Juárez in the state of Oaxaca, some 4,000 to 5,000 feet above sea level. Many residents of the district call their region the Rincón (the Corner). Most of them speak both Zapotec and Spanish. The native tongue of one village is Mixe. Natives of the *cabecera* (the district seat), San Ildefonso de Villa Alta, speak only Spanish.

I was the first anthropologist to undertake long-term field research in San Ildefonso de Villa Alta and its marketplace region, which includes thirteen villages. No extensive historical record existed of the political, legal, social, and economic development of the villages, and no discoverable contemporary social and cultural data had been recorded. Some schoolteachers, as part of their degree requirements, had prepared brief studies of village lives and histories, but the studies I was able to obtain were often contradictory. Thus I began my research with little localized contemporary data except studies by Nader (1964, 1965, 1966, 1969a), Nader and Metzger (1963), and de la Fuente (1949) of three villages in the Villa Alta district which were outside my study area.

The names Villa Alta and Villalteco have referred over time to many different Oaxacan groups. Villa Alta has been the name of a Sierra district and subprefecture that has varied in size from 110 *pueblos* in 1580 (Chance 1978a) to today's 25 *municipios* and their attached *agencias*.[2]

Villa Alta was a seat of Spanish intervention in relations among Mixe, Zapotec, and Chinantec villages of the Sierra. Histories of Oaxaca cite San Ildefonso de Villa Alta, founded in 1526, as one of the first Spanish settlements in this region of Mexico, along with Antequera (Oaxaca City) and Villa Baja (Tuxtepec). Villaltecos were the initial Spanish settlers in the Rincón, and Villa Alta was the first mestizo village among the Nexitzo-speaking Zapotec who worshipped the gods of Monte Albán, the ancient Zapotec capital in the Valley of Oaxaca, not far from the present-day Oaxaca City. Villaltecos, seekers of the Sierra's mineral wealth and Dominican messengers of Catholicism, were also keepers of the peace between Zapotec villagers and the Mixe soldiers of the Rey Condoyac, who ruled beneath the sacred peak of Zempoatépetl, when the Mixe sought conquest among the Zapotec of Zoogocho and their neighbors in 1570. The term *Villalteco* has also been used to designate the Zapotec (also termed Caxonos) spoken in the Sierra region of Yalálag (Nader 1969b, Whitecotton 1977). In this book, the term refers to persons residing in the district seat as well as to those who have migrated to urban communities or other areas.

Since its early years as both a Spanish and urban outpost, Villa Alta has played only a small role in the history of the Sierra. Chance (1978a, p. 53) noted that Villa Alta did not become an important Oaxacan settlement. Sierra villages such as Ixtlán, Ixtepejei, Yalálag, and Zacatepec have played larger roles in the waves of political, religious, and economic change that have swept through Oaxaca and the Sierra de Juárez (de la Fuente 1949, Kearney 1972, Laviada 1978).

As a marketplace, Villa Alta is the host of a small Monday *plaza* where, until recently, primarily intervillage rather than urban-village exchanges took place. Marketplaces of the district villages of Yaée, Zoogocho, and Yalálag are much larger. Villa Alta's nearest neighbors are among the poorest villages of the district and of Oaxaca. Not until 1984 did a reliable dirt road for motorized travel reach Villa Alta. An earlier road from Yalálag, completed in 1974, lacked bridges and therefore became impassable during the rainy season. Chance (1978b, p. iv) called the area "one of the most remote, inaccessible, and least acculturated of southern Mesoamerica."[3]

The village, as the seat of the district, hosts several state offices, including the state district court, the Juzgado Mixto de Primera Instancia. Villa Alta has been an administrative center for the Sierra territory since 1529, when an *alcaldía mayor* was established in the barrio of Analco. The village's historical significance lies in its role as both an outpost for the central governments and as a provincial center of economic, political, and cultural commerce, some of which passed through Villa Alta from Oaxaca City to regions of Veracruz and the Gulf Coast. Lemoine (1966) described Villa Alta of the eighteenth and early nineteenth centuries, prior to Mexico's independence, as one of Oaxaca's richest centers for trade in cochineal, the insects used in the production of a red dye that was popular in Europe. Although villages of the district were once rich in tribute for colonial officials and traders, Villa Alta was more a place to visit than to put down roots.

Villa Alta's resident population, it appears, never grew to rival the populations of its larger neighbors—Temazcalapa and Lachirioag. In 1571, resident Villaltecos numbered about thirty. In the middle of the eighteenth century some fifty-five families resided in the seat; in 1883 there were 538; and in 1950, 755 (Lemoine 1966). In 1984, by my count, there were 572 full-time residents.[4]

Villa Alta never regained its role as a crossroad for the exploiters of the Sierra's resources and cheap labor. The village has provided little intrigue for social scientists or historians. Its primary resource in data has been criminal and civil cases housed in the Juzgado Mixto de Primera Instancia. The cases cover periods from the sixteenth century to the present.[5] Now, few Zapotec villagers bring their conflicts and disputes and thus their tribute to this former seat of the alcalde mayor.

Nader (1969, p. 73) accurately reported the Zapotec view of the district seat in quoting a Taleano: "Better our treasury should flourish than that of Villa Alta."

Villa Alta was never a large village nor itself a center of production. However, it has retained, over time, a character best captured by Lemoine (1966, p. 195) who described the early Spanish settlement and its environs as a center of painful culture contact and dispute where, as a result of the military necessities of the colonial government and trade, people of various origins—the Spanish, Mexicans, and Tlaxcaltecos and the Zapotec, Mixe, and Mixtec Indians of Oaxaca— were forced for several centuries to live together. According to Lemoine (p. 195), the village Villa Alta became a "small Babylon."

The Villaltecos of today come from Zacatepec and other villages in the Mixe district, from the Chinantec and Zapotec villages in the Choapan district, from the Zapotec villages of Yalahui, Taguí, Roayaga, and from other villages in the Villa Alta district. They are descendants of the Spanish and Tlaxcalteco settlers of Villa Alta and the mestizos of Mixe Totontepec. They are the second and third generations of families from Oaxaca City who moved to Villa Alta in the 1920s, replacing Spanish-speaking silver workers and bureaucrats who left the district seat when the mines of Santa Gertrudis, Tabaa, and Mineral de Natividad shut down and revolution spread into the Sierra de Juárez. They are the grandchildren of bandits from Veracruz, murderers who have served time in the district jail (and others who have not), and refugees from guerrilla warfare in Guerrero. They are *viajeros* (itinerant merchants) and landless Zapotecs who sought a new life as storekeepers and day laborers (*jornaleros*). They are liberals and conservatives still fighting the religious and political battles of La Reforma. They are lawyers, politicians, teachers, telegraph operators, priests, merchants, doctors, and graduate students who have moved from dirt-floored adobe homes to large two-story, single-family dwellings in Oaxaca, Mexico City, Guadalajara, and Tijuana. They are goatherds and *minifundistas* (small landowners) who plant a steep half-acre of maize with nothing more than a hoe. They are village postal workers who read an encyclopedia during their breaks, telegraph operators who buy classical records with surplus income, and *mozos* (porters) who seek respite in a bottle of *aguardiente* from back-breaking work in the hot sun. They are *caciques* (political bosses), brokers, and moneylenders who have wielded power and exercised influence in Villa Alta and many neighboring villages.

Over the centuries since Villa Alta was founded, its importance as a headquarters village for politicians who captured the reins of state control has diminished. Nevertheless, the boundaries of the village have expanded into Mexico's urban capitals through emigration as its natives entered into both the modern capitalist economy and the expanding bureaucracies of the state and federal governments. Villa Alta, as a *municipio libre*, has become a modern open corporate community.[6] It has changed from an isolated village invaded by the forces of centralized control and economies to a stratified administrative center with components in urban centers and marketplaces. And, unlike modern migrants of the United States, urban Villaltecos continue to participate in the politics, conflicts, disputes, and economy of their native village. Villa Alta's Zapotec peasant neighbors have followed similar patterns but from different socioeconomic foundations. Historically, their villages have been less open than Villa Alta, and less stratified. But like Villaltecos, they have growing ties to state and national capitals as villagers migrate. In contrast to Villaltecos, they also have over the past ten years established new alliances with other villages of the region and with new centralized religious institutions.

Now, as in 1570, Villa Alta is at the crossroads of conflict between forces of change and tradition. Political and religious movements are sweeping over the Sierra de Juárez. They are met in forces of tradition that have preserved village-based religious and civil systems through the Colonial epoch and into the present. How the forces of the past and present come together through the development of village disputes is the subject of this book.[7]

The primary principles of organization underlying and guiding the legal processes of all these villages are the village and the divided village. These principles of organization largely determine the inhabitants' responses to internal disputes. The village is a goal to be achieved through legal processes, while the divided village is a condition to be avoided or repaired.

Like other principles such as equality and fairness, the village is omnipresent in the development and maintenance of relations in all fields of endeavor and interaction in these villages. It is the primary basis for evaluating relationships. The boundaries of the village as a principle do not correspond to the boundaries of the village as a political unit, which is limited by geography and membership criteria. As a principle of organization, the village may extend into a wide range of social action, even into activities that are not indigenous to the social and cultural past or present of the village as a political unit.

These villages put high value on participatory democracy. Major events in the enactment of participatory democracy are the *juntas* (meetings) of village citizens to discuss issues and participate in decisions concerning the maintenance processes of the village and its institutions. Most villages confine junta participation to adult males, although adult females now participate in some juntas in the district seat. The village concept says that decisions made by authorities should represent the *voz pública* (public voice, or voice of the people) and juntas are the formal processes through which these voices are heard.

Those who have the duty or obligation to give allegiance to the village and voluntary service through participation in local civil-religious organization are those who reside within the geographic boundaries of the village. In exchange, they receive, at the minimum, protection of their rights by village-based authority. In most cases, those born in the village maintain a lifetime right to participate in village decision-making processes, no matter where they reside, and villages actively encourage those who have moved to urban areas to continue to participate. Since these villages value allegiance and local control, an appeal by disputants to agencies of the external world, such as state courts, would violate the village principle.

As for the divided village, it is the antithesis of the village concept. It symbolizes challenges to all the values represented by the village. Two district villages—Betaza and Yalálag—are well known as historically divided villages. De la Fuente (1949) discussed the division of Yalálag into politically competitive barrios. Both villages have influenced the historical concept of the divided village as a breeding ground for violence and for the breakdown of local control.[8]

Many of Mexico's major historical conflicts are voiced in the disputes that I have seen unfold in Villa Alta. Behind each is a pentimento etched in generations and in ethnicity. Conquest, independence, reform, and revolution have left residues of difference in the community and its marketplace region. Ethnic and political characteristics distinguish Villa Alta from its Zapotec neighbors and create distance between them. The most significant differences have developed from Villa Alta's role as a headquarters village for the forces of centralization. Spanish-speaking Villaltecos, who have developed contacts with urban and state marketplaces, have managed many of the resources that have either filtered into the Rincón from Oaxaca City or are produced in the Villa Alta marketplace region. As a small plaza for both the bulking and the redistribution of dry goods and cash crops and as an administrative center for the collection and dissemination of information, Villa Alta has provided its residents with educational and entrepreneurial opportunities in the developing state bureaucracies and the capitalist economy.

What is important about the history of Villa Alta is the way in which it has been incorporated into village life. Power struggles between leaders of different generations and families and between local occupational and ethnic groups have captured and retained the themes of conflict dominant in various periods of Mexican history. Population shifts in the village have corresponded to broader political and economic changes. Villaltecos collect and preserve the past in local identities. The conservative nature of the village, as a receptacle rather than a generator of economic and occupational opportunities, has allowed local stratification within a narrow range of difference. Persons with wealth cannot afford to escape the consequences of local conflict. Those who are poor can become economic entrepreneurs who move upward into statuses that provide rewarding political contacts and patronage.

The most important characteristic that has distinguished development in the village of Villa Alta from that of its marketplace neighbors has been the overlap of administrative and economic brokerage. All of Villa Alta's large landholders have at least two sources of income. These *latifundistas* are also either owners of stores that sell dry goods, employees in state district bureaucracies, schoolteachers, or moneylenders. The major source of local wealth is coffee, a cash crop, introduced into the Rincón in the late 1860s (Perez García 1959, p. 274). Coffee yields fluctuate with the weather, the use and misuse of technology that nurtures the plant through periods of maturation, and the availability of day laborers. Profits and losses vary with market prices, local inflation, and the demands of local labor. Inflation and wages are affected by local economic and political factors, which are components of relations between Villalteco patrons and clients and between Villa Alta and its marketplace neighbors.

Salaries and mercantile income provide a stop-gap for Villaltecos as coffee prices fluctuate in response to larger market forces. These villagers have used their second incomes to purchase land from persons in debt, increase their coffee holdings, and apply technology to cultivation (nurseries, fertilization, and irrigation). As farmers in both Villa Alta and its marketplace region have fallen on hard times, they have turned to the seat's merchant-brokers and moneylenders for loans and credit. The extension of loans and credit has in turn ensured the future clientage of farmers and a reliable pool of day laborers essential to the Villalteco coffee harvest. Villaltecos have invested their greater and more secure surpluses in the education of their children, many of whom have entered into salaried occupations and some of whom have become lawyers and government officials. Children with nonagricultural incomes contribute to the income of their parents. Some provide their parents with important political ties.

In the Zapotec market system (Beals 1967, 1975), the Villa Alta marketplace is relatively small. The flow of income through its state district offices is the slowest of all Oaxaca district seats. Nevertheless, the presence of marketing and administration has been sufficient to generate significant differences between the stratification of Villa Alta and its marketplace neighbors. For the present population of Villa Alta, this process began in the 1920s and 1930s as federal programs in education reached into district villages (Spanish-speaking Villaltecos became teachers and teachers moved to the district seat). Villaltecos assumed control of state district offices, which they used for personal gain. The process slowed for some Villaltecos in the 1950s with the professionalization of district offices and accelerated for others with the elimination of nearby Lachirioag as a competitive plaza. These changes resulted in a shift in sources of income and brokerage and contributed to a shift in local political control.

The second shift occurred in the middle 1970s as the state stepped up its participation in the local economy by establishing the Comisión del Compra de Café and the regional CONASUPO (Compañía Nacional de Subsistencias Populares), stores that sell dry goods and beans and maize imported from outside the region at government-subsidized prices. The coffee commission broke patron-client ties between Villalteco coffee buyers and local producers. The CONASUPO weakened relations between Villaltecos and their Zapotec neighbors. Again, political control of the seat changed hands.

Between 1974 and 1984 several factors contributed to changes in seat politics. The offspring of Zapotec and Mixe villagers who moved to the seat in the 1950s multiplied and matured. The offspring of native Villaltecos matured and entered into urban occupations. Marketplaces in Lachirioag and Camotlán continued to atrophy, and in 1982 the road was completed from Oaxaca City through the Mixe district to Villa Alta.

Villa Alta became the sole regional marketplace, the end of the road for goods that traveled overland from Oaxaca City. Older Villaltecos moved to urban centers to join their now married and employed offspring, taking with them school-age children. A new wave of Zapotec and Mixe migration filled abandoned Villalteco houses. But these immigrants, unlike those of the 1950s, were workers at the new technical school and entrepreneurs. Immigrants and Villalteco farmers opened dry goods stores, bars, and small restaurants (*fondas*) that competed with those of established Villalteco merchants who could no longer secure a large clientele through loans and credit. The local market grew more open to competition.

In 1973 Emilio Zaragoza was a *campesino* (farmer) and a village drunk. He was a frequent visitor to the village jail for public disorderliness and lost days in the fields working off his sentences of public service. In 1974 one of his sons completed secondary school in Villa Alta and moved to Mexico City, where he found salaried employment. Another son, a telegraph operator in Oaxaca City, began to move into higher-paying positions. His daughter also found employment as an urban telegraph operator. His three children began to send him portions of their income. He was able to open a small cantina and dry goods store. By 1984 he had stopped drinking, was deriving his entire income from his cantina and his children, and was an important contributor to the fiesta of the Santo Intierro.

In 1973 Eduardo Vargas was a minifundista who lived in a small one-room adobe house in Taguí with his wife and three children. His father-in-law was a viajero and minifundista also based in Taguí. One of his brothers-in-law found employment that year as a teacher in Roayaga and the other left for northern Mexico to seek his fortune. By 1984 Vargas and the families of his father-in-law and brothers-in-law were all living in Villa Alta. Vargas was a custodian at the technical school, his father-in-law was a merchant in Oaxaca City and Villa Alta, the one brother-in-law was still a teacher in Roayaga, and the other was a Villalteco entrepreneur in liquor sales and entertainment. They founded one of Villa Alta's newest and largest family compounds.

In 1973 Urbano Bautista was a schoolteacher from Lachichina who had moved to Villa Alta when he married a Villalteca. He had seven children. Two were employed in Oaxaca City and Mexico City as telegraph operators and the others were in school in Villa Alta. In 1974 Bautista's oldest son returned with his family to Villa Alta to head the local telegraph office. By 1984 Bautista and his oldest son were co-owners of a two-story building, which they rented as an apartment and office space. Two other children had found employment and contributed to the family income. Bautista had moved to Oaxaca City, where he lived with three children. He rented his home in Villa Alta to state employees.

These are typical stories about the people of Villa Alta in the 1980s—but not about their Zapotec neighbors. The underlying economic structure for the differences between them lies in Villa Alta's role as a center for bulking and distribution in a dendritic market system. Kelley (1976) outlined the characteristics of such a system:

1) a hierarchy of commercial centers lacking interstitial placement of levels, often showing instead descending level with increasing distance from the highest-level center; (2) more low-level centers than predicted by the central-place model; (3) orientation of each lower-level center to only one center in the next level rather than two or three, as in the central-place model; (4) a

draining of hinterland population, income, or resources by the highest-level center; and (5) concentration of a political elite in a single high-level center, which is also the most important economic center.[9]

Marketplaces in the district that have had the advantage of overland communication with Oaxaca City are larger than the marketplace of Villa Alta. The villages that participate in them generally are wealthier in surplus. These marketplaces, located in Zoogocho, Yaée, Talea, and Yalálag, are rendered inaccessible to villagers of the Villa Alta marketplace region by distance, steep mountain banks, and the absence of local surplus for the purchase of cargo-carrying animals.

The thirteen villages of Villa Alta's marketplace region are widely scattered. Some are eight hours by foot from the district seat. This factor, along with the absence of large dry-goods stores in the villages, rendered it useful to the regional population to have three marketplaces on different days, in Camotlán, Lachirioag, and Villa Alta. Political opposition to Villa Alta also made the Zapotec marketplaces attractive to many villagers. Lachirioag lost its Monday market to Villa Alta in a court battle in the mid-1950s and was forced to shift to Thursday. The completion of the road to Villa Alta in 1982, even though it passed through Lachirioag, weakened the Lachirioag market further as viajeros found the market better among the wealthier Villaltecos. Extension of the road to Camotlán from Villa Alta in 1983 brought distant villages closer to the seat.

The drain of population and resources to higher-level centers was evident in population shifts during the period from 1974 to 1984 as Villaltecos moved to Oaxaca City, and Zapotec entrepreneurs moved to Villa Alta. Villa Alta has been the door to economic and occupational opportunities in the region, while cultural and historical differences handed the key to Villaltecos. Urban Villaltecos provided another important contemporary factor in continued Villalteco control over opportunities.

Orellana S. (1973) recorded similar observations of a village in Oaxaca's Mixteca Alta, which maintained a political hierarchy among emigrants to Mexico City that mirrored the village hierarchy. These urban villagers actively participated in village government and financed most village improvements. Although Beals found this case atypical, Orellana's account of the political and economic roles of the migrant Mixtecan urban association could apply, with some qualifications, to the present working of Villalteco politics and fiesta economies. Betaza also is controlled politically by shopkeepers in Oaxaca City. Lachirioag maintains political hierarchies in Oaxaca City and Mexico

City, where urban villagers meet to discuss and participate in village political decisions. Migrants from Talea residing in Oaxaca and Mexico City offer both political and financial support to the realization of village projects (Hirabayashi 1983). Urban Villaltecos in Oaxaca City and Mexico City are organized politically around opposed village political groups, the Caleros and Progressives. They also form committees for annual village fiestas, in addition to the contributions they make to family members still residing in the seat.

Urban Villaltecos are increasingly important to the village economy. As Villa Alta's marketplace has grown to include more viajeros and its dry goods stores have multiplied, Zapotec villagers have decreased their participation as vendors in the Villa Alta plaza and as clients of established Villalteco merchants. The coffee-growing Villaltecos depend on their neighbors for such staples as quality beans, chili peppers, herbs, quality maize, onions, and avocados. These local items are now scarce in Villa Alta, though they are abundant in nearby Lachirioag and Yatée.

As a result of the work of the Comisión del Compra de Café, more land in Temazcalapa, Taguí, Yetzecovi, and Yetzelalag is being converted to coffee cultivation.[10] The rise in the number of Villa Alta's Zapotec and Mixe entrepreneurs has provided alternative patrons to Zapotec villagers. *Compadres* and patrons are the first to bid on valued surpluses from regional villages. More marketplace goods are sold through personal channels. Villaltecos have turned to stores, where merchant prices are high, rather than to the marketplace for foodstuffs.

A new municipal building and marketplace and the proliferating dry-goods stores and fondas have been built on dreams that may not be fulfilled. As the familial, civil, capitalist, and fiesta economies of Villa Alta are becoming increasingly dependent on local coffee cultivation and urban salaries, the Zapotec of the region are constructing political, civil, and religious by-ways that do not pass through the district seat. Through regional assemblies that have developed over the past ten years, Zapotec villages now share political alliances and economic reserves to challenge the role of the state and of Villaltecos as the political elite.[11] Through Protestant assemblies that now encompass almost half the population of seven villages in the marketplace region and most of the population of Taguí, Zapotec villagers have withdrawn from both the fiesta and civil economies of their villages and established cross-village alliances, and they look toward Oaxaca City for both political and religious guidance. As state and urban funds flow into Villa Alta, regional and Protestant assemblies, both of which are indigenous movements, are constructing countercurrents to the seat's continued development as a marketplace, an administrative center, and a regional base for the dissemination of religious doctrine.

Mexico's economic crisis contributes to political and religious strains in the region.[12] Local annual inflation is estimated at 60 percent, with some prices rising daily. Villagers voice fears about government conscription of labor to aid in the pay-back of Mexico's international debts. Economic strains lend common sense to Protestant conversions: Protestants need not spend their surpluses on religious fiestas (*mayordomías*). Rather, they receive contributions from Protestant churches elsewhere. As a counterpoint to the religious changes, a major goal of the regional assemblies is to preserve and reconstruct traditional village civil-religious hierarchies that have deteriorated under Protestant conversions and economic pressures.

Zapotec opposition to Villa Alta is not new, although intervillage alliances may be a development of the past ten years. The Zapotec villages of the region were not active forces in Mexico's War of Independence or its Revolution (Nader 1969, Perez García 1956). Such organizations as the CNC (Congreso Nacional Campesino) have not been active forces among them, although the CNC has played an important role in the organization of Mixe villages (Laviada 1978). The villages of the Villa Alta marketplace region, in reference to Wolf's (1955) classification of peasant corporate communities along a continuum from "closed" to "open," have been closed in relation to politics, law, and marriage. (They tend toward endogamy, though exogamy is not prohibited.) Only in relation to their participation in state and national economies (now through cash-cropping) have they been classified as "open" (Beals 1975, p. 13).

Cultural differences are an important component of Zapotec opposition to and avoidance of Villa Alta. Though written histories of Villa Alta suggest that the Spanish were settlers on uninhabited land between Zapotec villages of the Rincón and the Mixe village of Totontepec, a "secret" of Villa Alta's marketplace neighbors is that the Zapotec village of Lachiwizi, with a population of 3,000, was located on the present site of Villa Alta when the Spanish arrived. Lachiwizi was decimated by European diseases, say the Zapotec, and the remaining villagers moved to the Villa Alta barrio of Analco and settled with Tlaxcalteco families, who accompanied the Spanish into the region and fought with them against Mixe invasions.

Though there appears to be no reference to Lachiwizi in historical records of the region, the Zapotec believe that the land of Villa Alta belongs to them. From this land the resources of the region have been exploited by both the Spanish and the Mexicans and by local caciques. Perez García (1956, vol. 1, pp. 63–72; Nader 1969) cited a document from the Juzgado Mixto de Primera Instancia in Villa Alta that suggests that representatives of some district villages sought an audience with Cortés, during which they presented him with tribute, asked to become Christians, and requested that he bring his religion into their land. Although representatives of such villages as Yaée, Talea, Lalopa, and Solaga were among these Zapotec messengers, only representatives from Betaza in the Villa Alta marketplace region joined them.

Perez García (1956, vol. 1, pp. 78–79) recounted that in 1660 the king of the Zapotec, Congun, united with Condoique, king of the Mixe, to overthrow the *alcalde mayor* of Villa Alta and other Spanish settlers. The two caciques were backed by twenty pueblos, but evidently were vanquished in their efforts. Since the Conquest and the settling of Villa Alta in 1526, residents of the district seat appear to have used the resources of the region with little local resistance.

Certainly, the mineral wealth of the Rincón attracted the Spanish to Villa Alta as much as their desire for peace between the Mixe and the Zapotec. From the eighteenth century to the early twentieth century and the Revolution, gold and silver mines were located in the district villages of Talea, Tabaa, Solaga, and Tanetze. During the Colonial period, an alcalde mayor of Villa Alta owned and operated a mine in the now abandoned village of Xaca (Perez García 1956, vol. 1, p. 264). According to Perez García exploitation of the mines was interrupted by the War of Independence, then resumed in 1825 under the British Compañía Minera Mexicana. The extraction of minerals ended around 1908 as the Revolution reached the Sierra (Perez García 1956, vol. 1, p. 270).

Although written histories of Villa Alta are scarce, it appears that Villaltecos and their neighbors participated little in the battles of La Reforma, the French intervention, the civil strife, and the Mexican Revolution of the latter half of the nineteenth century and the early twentieth century.[13] Other Oaxaqueños—the Mexican Presidents Benito Juárez and Porfirio Díaz and the generals from Ixtlán and Ixtepeji, Francisco Meixueiro and Fidencio Hernández—grabbed center stage in the making of Sierra history. An armed group of Villaltecos, led by a renegade friar (Berry 1981, p. 73) and shouting *"Viva la religion,"* captured the cabecera in 1860 during the War of Reform, which initiated the separation of church and state. The group included the ancestors of two current Villalteco caciques. The governor of Oaxaca dispatched a young leader from Ixtlán, Francisco Meixuerio (from whom Villa Alta's former *mero cacique* [top political boss] Raul Torres traces descent) to contain and extinguish the rebellion, which he did quickly (Perez García 1956, vol. 2, p. 24).

Like the telling of much Mexican history, the historical tales that live in the memories of Villaltecos focus on individuals and their abilities to control and create events. Those who occupy the imaginations of Villaltecos began to arrive in the cabecera during the latter half of the nineteenth century, most during the 1920s and 1930s following the Revolution. During these periods some Spanish families of Villa Alta left the seat. Others, like the silver-working grandparents of the Fabelas, stayed. The end of easily accessible mineral wealth certainly hastened the abandonment of Villa Alta, as did political reforms. Federal participation in district education, which began in the 1920s, brought Spanish-speaking teachers, including the young Raul Torres, to Villa Alta. Others, already there, like the Fabelas, found employment as teachers and telegraph operators. (Telegraph service was established in Villa Alta around the turn of the century.) Two lines of Blascos arrived from Oaxaca City as employees. The Mendioleas returned to Villa Alta from Mixe-mestizo Totontepec. Torres, the Fabelas, the Blascos, and the Mendioleas will figure largely in this study.

The cultivation of coffee gave the new residents a reason to establish their homes in Villa Alta, and their salaries gave them the means to accumulate land. Teachers who worked and became political advisers in Zapotec and Mixe villages, though often absent from Villa Alta, maintained their families in the district seat. Villaltecos of the next generation were to increase their participation as individuals in the governing of villages in the marketplace region through positions as primary schoolteachers. Some, including the brother of Raul Torres, who is the wealthiest landholder in Villa Alta, neglected their salaried positions to remain in Villa Alta and tend to prospering coffee fields. Some teachers, including Areli Fabela and David Sesto, won support in the villages where they taught; others alienated villagers by neglecting their duties, drinking, and reporting local offenses to the district court—a violation of the village ethic.

The district court was my reason for beginning research in Villa Alta in 1973.[14] Laura Nader, who had studied dispute settlement in local courts of the district villages of Talea de Castro and Juquila Vijanos, suggested that I focus on the Oaxaca state legal system, to which these villages could appeal their disputes.

As I collected cases from the district court in Villa Alta, observed its proceedings, and sought integration into the social and family life of the district seat, I became aware of a legal system operating in tandem with that of the state. Most village disputes prosecuted by the state in the Juzgado, including cases initiated by the elected governments of the district's municipios libres, ended abruptly as the flow of information from the village to the state court ended (Parnell 1978a, 1978b). The politically unaligned villages of the district had independently developed similar strategies to limit state participation in local conflicts and disputes. They shared the ethic of local control.

Variations in village size, proximity to the court in Villa Alta, and economic development did not appear to influence the frequency with which villagers appealed disputes to the state. The only factors that influenced village cohesiveness, such as a political division in Yalálag (de la Fuente, 1949), weakened the abilities of villagers and village governments to cooperate in befuddling district court officials and resisting state investigations into local disputes. Their efforts were aided by Oaxaca's limited resources for salaries and both criminal and civil prosecution in the outposts of its poorer districts.

I gathered the materials for my analysis during two separate periods of field research: eighteen months in 1973–74 and six months in 1984. The research included participant observation, structured and unstructured interviews and conversations, a household composition census I conducted in the district seat, and case documents gathered from district court archives. I checked the impressions I developed while working in the seat by traveling to most villages in the marketplace regions of Villa Alta, Camotlán, Yaée, and Talea. I also lived in the exceptional village of Taguí, at that time the only Zapotec village with a sizable Protestant population (about fifty percent Jehovah's Witnesses) to search for exceptions to the patterns of disputing that were taking shape.

Two factors had a strong influence on the nature of the materials I gathered while looking into the contexts of the district court. First, I was an active participant in the life of the village of Villa Alta. The village government required that I fulfill, like all other residents who were not state government employees stationed in Villa Alta, the duties of a household head. These duties included participating in village work projects, meetings, and committees. Second, I used a wide variety of informants rather than just one. This factor was dictated by the nature of Villalteco life—its pluralism and partisan politics.

My active participation in village life eventually led to my entrance into Villalteco information networks. I learned that they are an important component of a more extensive informal legal system than I had imagined. It may be difficult for anyone who has not conducted field

work in a village society to believe that such a small community could in
any coordinated fashion conceal large amounts of spoken information
from someone who was living among them and eagerly and actively
seeking their information. The abilities of villagers and tribesmen to
both conceal and fabricate information is the tale of many anthropologists.

Villaltecos historically are brokers of information between peasants
and bureaucracies. They have also managed to maintain an autonomous village politic in the presence of state bureaucrats and legal
officials. Some Villaltecos manage the contradictory loyalties of bureaucrat and villager. When I began to receive the gift of insider
information in exchange for my services to the village, I began to see
how Villaltecos juxtaposed their village, the region, and the state. To
regulate the role of the anthropologist in their community, Villaltecos
applied the procedural rules through which they have extended the
village legal system beyond local everyday disputes between husbands,
wives, and neighbors to include a much larger slice of Mexican national
life. As I had been looking for one form of law, another form of law had
concealed it.

The major turning point in my study came during my ninth month
in Villa Alta, when I was working on the church committee for the
fiesta of the Santo Intierro. Just before the fiesta began a cacique was
murdered. The district seat went into mourning. Because I had talked
frequently with this man and had often visited with members of his
family, Villaltecos felt I deserved to be involved in discussions of the
murder and of the man's life. As one informant said, by that time I had
earned the right to engage in the sharing of information about Villa
Alta and Villaltecos. The extended case of assassination (Parnell
1978b), one that still remains unresolved for many Villaltecos, revealed
information about many other disputes and opened the door to knowledge about factional politics in the district seat. The murder was a
turning point for Villaltecos as well as for me; it precipitated their
political division into Caleros and Progressives.

My entrance into the informational processes of insiders provided
important knowledge of how Villaltecos controlled their village boundaries by creating and manipulating information. It revealed aspects of
district seat life about which I had learned little during my first nine
months of research.

In 1984, when I returned to Villa Alta for a second period of study, I
quickly discovered that getting information would be no problem.
Whereas ten years earlier I had to seek it out, I was now bombarded
with information about the state of the village and individuals within it.
It appeared that the political division itself and the movements within

district villages were generating information. To borrow a Villalteco saying, politics and religion were dancing in the mouths of the people.[15]

Colson (1974, p. 82) wrote, "If the anthropologist attempts . . . to describe the dynamic processes by which the community adjusts to changing circumstances, he concentrates upon particular political battles." In many ways this book is an extended case study (Epstein 1967, Parnell 1982). In chapter 2 I present the district seat disputes as they expanded and interlinked in 1984. In chapter 3 I examine pre-1984 disputes in the district seat in relation to politics, social organization, and social structure, and I attempt to place these earlier disputes in the larger context of social forces influencing life in the extended village. Then, based on the case presentation and background information, I analyze the 1984 disputes in chapter 4, examining their effects on the social lives of their participants and the role of the village within its social universe. Chapter 5 goes beyond the district seat to look at the way the other villages of the district were reacting to legal, religious, and political change. The final two chapters summarize my findings and relate them to the studies of other anthropologists.

Each chapter presents a facet of village law. Chapter 3 discusses the social matrix of the district seat in which disputes are bred and then become expanded as villagers explore their society. Chapter 4 analyzes disputing in the seat, first as a symbolic process of creating, evaluating, and juxtaposing various forms of village life and then as a practical process of negotiating a compromise among alternative structures of village relationships. Chapter 5 looks at how local conflicts in villages of the marketplace region have developed, through disputing, into regional political and religious alliances that function as negotiating teams in the construction of villager responses to change. Chapter 6 examines why villagers use the social resources of the village rather than those the state of Oaxaca provides to resolve their disputes. Chapter 7 then summarizes the dynamics of disputing in Villa Alta by relating the process of centralization to the process of disputing through a system of segmentary oppositions.

Disputing is an important component of the daily lives of Villaltecos. Through disputes they communicate their views, check up on one another, express their anger, and relieve the tensions bred in village conflicts. As the disputes of Villa Alta escalate beyond the dyadic relationships of neighbors, friends, and close kin to include a broader range of participants from the village, the region, and the city, they grow to encompass some of the major controversies and issues Mexico is facing today. At the same time, the interrelational context of escalating disputes provides villagers with the processes and symbols through which they can phrase those issues in relation to local concerns. Escalating disputes can also generate for their participants new elements of uncertainty as well as social arenas for innovation. Their outcomes are affected by the shifting alliances and old schisms of village, regional, and urban politics.

CHAPTER 2

The Case of the Padre's Keys

February 1984 in Villa Alta is a dry month of work and preparation for the fiestas and the planting that lie ahead.[1] Campesinos and jornaleros work in the fields picking mature red and yellow coffee beans. At nine on weekday mornings young children hurry to the primary school in the central square. Older children climb the steep slopes above the square to attend the secondary technical school.[2]

Members of the church and kitchen committees for the March fiesta of the Santo Intierro walk from house to house collecting money for the celebration. Appointed by the village president, the committee members are supporters of Juan Calero. Calero is the chief opponent of David Mendiolea, the mero cacique of Villa Alta. Calero and his ally, Alberto Negrete, spend one or two afternoons each week in consultation with the Catholic padre of Villa Alta.[3] They are often joined in the rectory by Ezekiel Zarco, who runs the post office, and his first cousin, who is employed in Villa Alta's telegraph office. Zarco heads the church committee.

The padre has served in the district seat and the villages in its marketplace region for almost three years. Relations between the padre and Mendiolea's Progressives are distant and antagonistic. They have quarreled over the padre's opposition to certain fiesta entertainments and his prohibitions against Villalteco traditions associated with marriage ceremonies and fifteenth birthdays. But the tension between the padre and the Progressives arises primarily from the former's close alignment with the Caleros and his participation in village politics. The padre dislikes most Villaltecos, who act like his equals, and prefers Villa Alta's Zapotec neighbors in the outlying villages.

Villa Alta's president, Otilio Espinosa, who in the past has wavered between the Caleros and the Progressives, but now aligns with the Progressive boss Mendiolea, welcomes into his home the padre's assistant, whom the people of Villa Alta call *el seminarista.* A young Mixe from the Zacatepec district and a friend of Espinosa's older son, the seminarian is a self-described pacifist who enjoys talking about the beauties of the mountains and about Mixe cultural traditions. Unlike the padre, the seminarian participates actively in Villa Alta's social life. He drinks with the men, attends dances, and visits the homes of Villalteco families, often in order to read stories to their younger children.

Early one February afternoon the seminarian and a friend, a man in his late teens who is a member of the fiesta church committee, walk from the central square to the home and cantina of Fernando Gomez. The two men order beer and begin to chat with Gomez. The chat extends into a late-afternoon discussion over several beers with four men from the Villa Alta district villages of Taguí and Camotlán who stop at the cantina on their way to another village.

While the men are drinking, the padre finds that the church keys are missing from his office. Worried, he wonders where the seminarian is. The *mayordoma,* Esperanza Blasco, who is at the church, tells him that the seminarian has been drinking at the cantina all afternoon.[4] The location of the keys is a matter of serious local concern. Two years before, a thief had taken religious objects from the church. The theft resulted in several accusations that appeared to be politically motivated, including some against David Mendiolea's mother, who was then the mayordoma. No accusations against individuals were substantiated, and no one was accused in either the village or the district court.

The padre walks to Gomez's cantina and asks the seminarian for the church keys. The seminarian says he does not have them. The padre doubts his word and the two argue. The padre leaves the cantina and walks to the office of the Ayuntamiento (the elected government) of Villa Alta on the central square. He tells President Espinosa that the seminarian will not give him the church keys and asks that he be brought to the municipal building and forced to surrender the keys. Espinosa goes to the corridor and blows a whistle to summon Villa Alta's six-member volunteer police force. He instructs the police to apprehend the seminarian at Gomez's cantina.

Word quickly reaches the cantina that Espinosa has summoned the police, and the seminarian flees before they arrive. They search for him in the houses and fields above the central square but he eludes them. Some of his friends object to the use of the police, for the seminarian, they claim, does not have the church keys. The next day the seminarian appears voluntarily in the central square and speaks with President Espinosa, who decides not to call for his jailing. The seminarian goes to a cantina on the central square and returns to drinking.

By now the confrontation between the padre and his assistant has become a subject of heated discussion in the voz pública (includes village gossip). Some women, active in the church, including the mayordoma, take the padre's side. In the dusty streets and crowded kitchens of the village, church women charge that the seminarian is not really a seminarian—that he lied about his identity. They claim that the padre says he is a phony who came to Villa Alta to turn the people against the Catholic church. They say the padre and the seminarian had once been friends; the padre had tried to educate the seminarian but had not been successful. The phony seminarian drinks too much, they say.

The next day, when the seminarian appears in the central square, some women and Calero supporters continue to share stories about his alleged past. They spread several tales, most of them concerning his visits to villages north of Villa Alta. Recently, they say, he attended the fiesta in Yetzecovi while the padre was visiting Oaxaca City; wearing the padre's robes, he gave mass, although he was not qualified to do so, and then seduced a young woman of the village.

Friends of the seminarian come to his defense. The padre, they say, sometimes argues with villagers in the cantinas and has even hit villagers in the heat of anger. He has little respect for the people of Villa Alta and their customs. He does not allow villagers to adorn the church for a wedding or participate in customary wedding ceremonies, saying that the customs of Villa Alta are foolish and take up too much time. The padre also charges for the masses he gives in other villages, they claim.

Through his superiors in Oaxaca City the padre soon arranges the seminarian's exit from Villa Alta. But, while persons influential in the church of Villa Alta have favored the padre in this conflict, damaging information has circulated about him. Not only have his actions against the seminarian angered President Espinosa, but the dispute has also involved Espinosa's supporters, the padre's Calero supporters, and the padre's Progressive opponents.

The seminarian leaves Villa Alta one week after the confrontation over the church keys, but the dispute continues to expand. The padre complains to Espinosa that the seminarian has taken some of the padre's money and clothes, his guitar, and his gun. The secretary of Villa Alta records the padre's complaint. Because the seminarian is no longer in Villa Alta, the secretary sends the case to the *ministerio público* (prosecutor) attached to the Juzgado Mixto de Primera Instancia, the state district court located in Villa Alta.

Information about the dispute continues to develop in the public voice. Friends of the seminarian argue that the padre lost his head at the cantina because he was jealous of the seminarian. The seminarian was qualified to offer mass, they claim, and the padre saw him as competition and wanted to get rid of him; the padre was also angry because the seminarian did not charge villages for the masses he performed.

The first week in March the seminarian returns to Villa Alta to present his testimony to the ministerio público. On the night of March 4 he joins some bureaucrats in a cantina, two doors above the house of Esperanza Blasco. There, well into his cups, the seminarian denies the charges that the padre has placed against him. He removes a 5,000-peso bill from his pocket and, in the presence of his drinking companions, tears it to shreds, claiming that money is not important to him and he has no need to steal.[5]

Three days later Tito Mendiolea, the district court recorder, informs his aunt, Esperanza Blasco, who has just finished her term as mayordoma, that President Espinosa and others in the Ayuntamiento have prepared an *escrito* (brief) to be sent to the padre's superiors in Oaxaca City, calling for the padre's removal from Villa Alta. The document claims that the padre purposely misinformed officials in the complaints he placed against the seminarian. Blasco passes this news on to the women in her network, including those most active in the Catholic church. Espinosa quickly denies that he signed the document. He claims that the district seat's police chief and the *síndico* (village prosecutor) wrote, signed, and sent the complaint to Oaxaca City.

In spite of Espinosa's attempt to dissociate himself from the dispute he has earned the opposition of the church women's network.[6] They now define the dispute as one between Espinosa and the padre. They attempt to move the case against the seminarian into the office of the judge of the district court and to influence the judge to favor the padre. The women's network also spreads word of the charges the padre made against the seminarian. Blasco and others who had been in the padre's rooms before the alleged thefts claim they had seen many of the objects he later said were missing—and that these items had indeed been among his possessions.

Supporters of the seminarian speak of how a year ago the padre angered the mero cacique, David Mendiolea, by forbidding dancing in the village on the Friday night of the fiesta of the Santo Intierro (the third Friday in March). Both Progressives and Caleros claim that the padre agreed to allow the dance only after Mendiolea promised him a cut of the proceeds from selling beer and brandy.

As the dispute spreads it pits many female supporters of the Progressives, including the former mayordomas Esperanza Blasco and the mother of David Mendiolea, against their political allies and their own families. Blasco is the mother-in-law of Urbano Estrada and the aunt of both Luis Vera and his wife, Sarah Blasco de Vera—all important allies of the padre's opponent, Mendiolea. Blasco's daughter, the wife of Urbano Estrada, is a supporter of the padre. Rosalinda Estrada, the daughter of Urbano, sides with her grandmother. Rosalinda has just married the son of a leading Calero lieutenant, and her new mother-in-law is a sister of Ezekiel Zarco, the Calero supporter.

Another of Zarco's sisters, Luisa, who is not married but has two children by bureaucrats no longer stationed in Villa Alta, is also a major supporter of the padre.[7] She is one of the most prodigious spreaders and retainers of information in Villa Alta, especially about sexual relations and parentage. Luisa is the new mayordoma, succeeding her aunt, Esperanza Blasco. She also has a new job working in Blasco's kitchen, although Blasco has few to feed—only the judge of the district court, the head of Villa Alta's telegraph office, and Tito Mendiolea, the district court recorder, who is Blasco's nephew.

Both Blasco and Luisa speak to the judge about the padre's case. They tell him the stories being passed in the public voice against the seminarian. The judge says the case is still in the hands of the ministerio público and he can do nothing until it is consigned to him.[8] The padre occasionally visits Blasco's kitchen for coffee. Whenever he arrives, the judge leaves and returns to his rented room in Tito Mendiolea's house.

One evening in March David Mendiolea arrives from Oaxaca City for one of his twice-monthly visits to Villa Alta. He stops into Blasco's kitchen for his usual chat about village events. Blasco generally assumes the role of wise elder during these talks, while the mero cacique shares his knowledge of village disputes and projects and also his views on them. Tito and Luisa are in Blasco's kitchen when Mendiolea arrives. Blasco presents her side of the dispute between the padre and the seminarian, arguing in subdued tones that the seminarian indeed robbed the padre. Mendiolea asks why, if she has knowledge concerning the robbery, she has not offered to testify before the ministerio público. Blasco leaves the room without responding. Luisa then places her arguments before the cacique but, like her aunt, terminates the discussion at the mention of being a witness in the case.

The fiesta of the Santo Intierro begins on the third Wednesday in March and lasts until the following Sunday. It is both a religious and a secular fiesta, involving events in the Catholic church as well as dances, performances by schoolchildren, fireworks, contests, and family get-togethers. For two weeks prior to the fiesta, the two groups responsible for preparing and conducting fiesta activities, the church and kitchen committees, meet early each morning and work into the evening.[9]

The dispute over the padre and the seminarian now becomes entwined with a confrontation between the Caleros and the Progressives over the conduct of the fiesta and the funds to finance it. The first direct confrontation occurs on a Wednesday, two weeks before the fiesta is to begin. The head of the church committee, Ezekiel Zarco, and his committee of eight meet with President Espinosa in his office to discuss their problems.

Zarco explains that the committee has been unable to raise sufficient funds through *cuotas* (quotas, or mandatory villager contributions) to pay Villa Alta's band the 20,000 pesos necessary to guarantee that it will play at all the major fiesta events—for a procession on the first night of the fiesta (*calenda*), in the central square during afternoons and mornings of the fiesta, and, the immediate problem, during *rosarios* (recitations) at the Catholic church each night for two weeks preceding the fiesta. The committee can afford to pay the band only 10,000 pesos. Zarco asks the president to provide the other 10,000 pesos from Ayuntamiento funds.

Quotas have been a source of disagreement between Espinosa and Zarco and Negrete. Last year quotas for the fiesta were 1,000 pesos for *empleados* (employees) and 500 pesos for campesinos. This year Zarco and Negrete have twice reduced the quotas. Now, two weeks before the fiesta, they are 400 pesos for empleados and 200 for campesinos. Several Progressives had complained that they did not wish to pay the high quotas—a side of the issue usually argued by Caleros. However, it is the Caleros who are collecting the money this time, and the Progressives remember past Calero resistance to fulfilling village obligations.

Zarco claims that more than half the Villa Alta residents who should pay the quota have not done so and many are refusing to pay. Action, such as jailing, can be taken against them later, but the immediate problem is that the committee has insufficient funds. Zarco's strategy is to ask wealthier Progressives to contribute more and reduce the hardship imposed on campesinos. Thus Zarco is seeking the cooperation of the very persons he has opposed for years.

Zarco also tells Espinosa that a conflict with the padre has not yet been resolved. The padre has prohibited dancing on the night of the third Friday in March, which is the third night of the fiesta and its most important religious day. Villagers favor holding a dance that night, as they did last year. Then, the president and David Mendiolea had told the padre that it was not appropriate for him to forbid anything that was to take place on village rather than church grounds. After the padre had agreed to allow the dance if half its proceeds were donated to the church, villagers had said that the padre was hypocritical, that is, his claim to religious considerations was merely a pretense for gaining financially from the village's fiesta.

Responding to Zarco's report, Espinosa says that it is the committee's responsibility to finance, schedule, and carry out fiesta events. As for the padre, Espinosa's talking to him about anything is a waste of time. Espinosa is aware that the people in the village say he signed the complaint against the padre that was sent to the bishop in Oaxaca City, but that is untrue. The president argues, as he did last year, that it is improper for the padre to intervene in the affairs of village governance. He suggests that the committee meet with the padre and talk him into dropping his opposition to the dance.[10]

A young entrepreneur who moved to Villa Alta from Taguí and married a Villalteca is present at this meeting. He has arranged for a band from Oaxaca City to play at the fiesta dances on Thursday, Friday, and Saturday evenings. He will charge admission and sell beer, soft drinks, and brandy, then pay the band from his proceeds. He argues that cancellation of one of these dances will leave insufficient profit to pay the band the fees they are asking.

In the matter of the Villa Alta band, Espinosa suggests that the committee meet with the band that evening at nine during their practice session. Espinosa says he will be there and they can all discuss whether or not the band is willing to play for less than 20,000 pesos. He also agrees to consider making a contribution to the band from Ayuntamiento funds. Zarco and his committee, along with the entrepreneur, then leave the president's office and walk across the central square to the Catholic church.

They enter the padre's office and stand together in a circle around his desk. Zarco tells him that the president and other villagers, including the committee, wish to hold the Friday evening dance and are seeking the padre's permission. The entrepreneur adds that if the band from Oaxaca City cannot play on Friday night they will probably not play at all. The padre is unswayed. He reiterates that for religious reasons he cannot allow dancing on the third Friday in March. He is not interested in gaining anything personally or financially by opposing the dance and suggests that the third dance be held on Wednesday or Sunday night. Zarco asks if the padre will change his mind, but the padre stands his ground.

Zarco and his committee then agree to go along with the padre's ban. They also agree to forbid Friday dances in private homes. Zarco sends a messenger to tell Espinosa that the committee has been unsuccessful and there will be no Friday dance.

At nine in the evening Zarco and his committee walk into the band's practice room above the municipal offices. President Espinosa arrives shortly afterward. Zarco and Espinosa do not leave the room until eleven. That evening will be the last time the two men speak to each other until after the fiesta. Espinosa is angry that Zarco and his committee gave in to the padre's demand.

Zarco presents his case to the band, citing his committee's lack of funds. He says the committee cannot compromise the band by asking it to play at all scheduled fiesta events while receiving only partial payment. He asks the president to help his committee by contributing funds from the Ayuntamiento. Espinosa responds angrily that Zarco, Negrete, and their committees were irresponsible in reducing fiesta quotas and did not make a sufficient effort to collect them. Such problems did not arise in the past, he says, and he will not contribute Ayuntamiento funds to help pay the band.

Zarco answers that the problem is indeed probably his fault and that he can only ask for the cooperation of the band in playing at fiesta events. He himself is from a humble background and cannot ask villagers to pay more when they cannot afford more. But even some salaried Progressives had opposed the higher quotas for the fiesta. Espinosa states again that the committees should raise the quotas to pay for fiesta events and not seek contributions from the government.

As Espinosa attacks Zarco, members of Zarco's committee walk out in anger. Zarco remains behind and asks the band to make a decision on the matter. Members of the band say that their president is not present and that they cannot reach a decision before discussing the matter with him. The band's vice-president says, however, that Zarco is right in concluding that since the committee cannot pay the entire 20,000 pesos it cannot compromise the band by expecting it to play at all scheduled events. Zarco joins his committee outside the practice room, where they agree that the president has not acted properly in refusing to allocate village funds.

The next morning the committee members meet in front of the church at seven, as they will do each morning for the next two weeks and during the five days of the fiesta. Each morning they water down and sweep the dirt grounds of the church and clean the exterior walls. They build platforms extending like terraces from the floor nearly to the ceiling of the church, just below the glass-encased life-sized figure of San Ildefonso, the patron saint of Villa Alta. The terraces are made from tables and boxes and are covered with white cotton cloth. The committee members move life-sized figures of saints from their alcoves in the church to the terraces and place among them large candles in chrome holders.

The larger than life-sized figure of the black Santo Intierro is removed from its glass case above the altar of the church and placed on a table in front of the terraces.[11] Just below the altar a smaller image of the Santo Intierro lies encased in a glass box atop a wooden table. Large candles are placed throughout the church, and on the Thursday of the fiesta, flowers will arrive from Oaxaca City. Women will place them in large chrome vases among the candles and figures of saints on the terraces.

In the afternoons before the fiesta, the committee members prepare the *palo encerado,* a tall pine trunk shaved smooth and covered with wax. During the fiesta they will place it in a large hole above the central square. Whoever climbs it first will take home the prizes he can gather from a wooden frame at the top of the trunk.

The committee members attempt to resolve their financial problems. They go to bureaucrats and seek contributions from them or their offices. The *ministerio público* gives 500 pesos from his petty cash drawer, and the office of the Comisión del Compra de Café gives 2,000 pesos for the purchase of a *torito*—sticks bent together in the shape of a bull's head and covered with firecrackers and sparkler wheels. Each night of the fiesta, in front of the secondary school, men and boys will place toritos on their heads, light the firecrackers, and chase the children of the village while the bulls crackle and spew fire.

Every evening for two weeks before the fiesta, committee members ring the church bells, announcing either mass or rosario. At seven o'clock villagers gather in the church and recite and sing to the accompaniment of the village band. When the mass or rosario is over the committee ignites firecrackers on the church grounds. Then the congregation files out of the church carrying lit candles and forms two single lines on each side of the small figure of the Santo Intierro encased in the glass box. Committee members carry the box and, with the congregation, follow the band around the church singing "*Santo Intierro te adoramos y pedimos tu perdón.*"

One week before the fiesta, representatives of the village's Mexico City committee arrive in Villa Alta. Each year an image of the Santo

Intierro is taken from Villa Alta to go from house to house in Oaxaca City or Mexico City. Village urbanites pay their city's village committee for the privilege of hosting the image in their homes. The urban village committee then allocates the contributions to specific events and projects for the fiesta of the Santo Intierro. The image has been housed in Mexico City homes since last April. Now the Mexico City committee has brought lights to Villa Alta to adorn the church and its yard. They decorate the central square park and contribute the gifts to be hung atop the palo encerado, including a 5,000-peso bill.

As the last members of the Mexico City committee arrive Zarco's church committee gathers in the post office to prepare an accounting of who has paid the quota and who has not. A list reveals that over half the taxable villagers still have quotas outstanding. Zarco and his committee then go to the corridor of the municipal building, where the Mexico City committee is attaching decorations to the strings of lights. Zarco gives the urbanites the same information he has placed before the president—the committee has insufficient funds to finance the fiesta.

Also present are Juan Calero and Tino Negrete of the kitchen committee, whose task is to feed the guest band for the fiesta. This year it is the highly praised band of the village of Zacatepec, seat of the neighboring Mixe district.[12] Like Zarco's committee, the kitchen committee has sought aid from President Espinosa in meeting their obligations. Espinosa has asked individual Villaltecos to pay for one of the band's meals or to invite the band to their homes to eat. Several Villaltecos have responded, including the mero cacique, David Mendiolea.

The urbanites give the same answer to both committees: If you are having financial problems, tell Mendiolea . . . he has money. Zarco then sends a messenger to request that Mendiolea meet with him in the corridor of the municipal building. Within moments Mendiolea is standing there with his opponents, the Caleros.

The discussion between Zarco and Mendiolea is just as heated as the one between Zarco and Espinosa had been. Zarco explains that the quotas will provide insufficient funds to finance the fiesta and asks Mendiolea to make up the difference. Mendiolea says he has already paid for one meal for the band as well as a torito. He suggests that Zarco call for a *sobrecuota*, or second quota, to be paid by all villagers to make up the difference between quotas collected and fiesta costs. Mendiolea argues angrily that it is not his responsibility to pay for the fiesta. If the villagers want a fiesta, they must be willing to pay for it. Mendiolea's response angers Zarco, but he does not reply in kind. He thanks

Mendiolea for his suggestions. After Mendiolea leaves, Zarco tells his committee that he will not raise quotas or impose a sobrecuota.

On Wednesday afternoon, the first day of the fiesta, the band of Zacatepec arrives by truck and disembarks at the ruins of the church of Analco, the first Spanish and Tlaxcalteco settlement in what is now the nucleated village of Villa Alta. The band is met by the church committee and President Espinosa. Also present from Oaxaca City and Mexico City are the sons of Raul Torres and David Sesto, former caciques. They are Calero leaders and lifelong opponents of Mendiolea. After Espinosa gives his welcoming speech one son of Torres and one son of Sesto also welcome the band. No Progressives other than Espinosa are present.

The band, after its maestro responds to the welcoming speeches, walks to the Villa Alta central square and enters the office of the president. There, sitting in chairs, the band serenades him. Then the band members go to the home of Jacobo Cartucho, in whose storeroom they are to sleep. Sitting at long tables they eat dinner with Cartucho and his mother.

The calenda that night is the first major event of the fiesta. The church committee, schoolchildren, and young men and women of the village gather in the churchyard at nine. The band of Zacatepec joins them. The Mexico City fiesta committee has prepared paper lanterns for the children to carry in the calenda. Each lantern glows with the light of a candle.

The calenda procession moves from house to house asking villagers to donate aguardiente, *mezcal,* or money to the fiesta. The aguardiente and mezcal will be served to the bands as they play at fiesta events, and the money will buy beer for them. Church committee members announce the arrival of the band by running ahead of the calenda and igniting firecrackers. Three committee members follow them, two to carry large plastic containers to collect the aguardiente and mezcal and one to knock on doors. As committee members approach a house, they shout "*Viva*" and the name of the head of the household, inviting someone to appear with contributions. The band often stops to play several numbers at the houses of respected villagers and their leaders. Those who wish to do so invite the band to play in their yards in exchange for beers and cups of aguardiente or mezcal. The men and women who have joined the procession dance to traditional tunes in the yards of the generous Villaltecos.[13]

The band passes by the houses of all the Progressive leaders. It stops only at the homes of the Caleros. It plays for an hour or so each at the homes of Raul Torres and David Sesto. When committee members knock on the doors of Progressive leaders, including David Mendiolea, they get no response. The fiesta of the Santo Intierro, one of the most important annual events of the village, has become a Calero fiesta, and the ruling Progressives have quietly withdrawn from participation.

The calenda ends at two the next morning in the central square. The band members retire to the storeroom of Jacobo Cartucho to sleep but find that there are no *petates* (straw mats used both for sleeping and for drying coffee).

Zarco and the church committee retire to his home to count the monetary donations from the calenda—nearly 5,000 pesos. Only now remembering the petates, Zarco sends the few he has collected to the storeroom with a committee member. Tell the band, he says, that there are no more petates because David Mendiolea, the man in the village with the most petates, refused to loan them to the committee.

Another event during the fiesta increases the animosity between Zarco and Espinosa. The village police are to help the church committee carry the heavy waxed palo to the central square, where it is to be grounded in a deep hole. Espinosa, however, orders the police not to help the committee. Without police help, but aided by Caleros from Mexico City, the committee attempts to raise the heavy pine trunk using ropes and supports made from branches. The raising takes more than an hour. The palo is secured insufficiently and will waver as young Villaltecos clamber up it; the Progressives will level criticism against Zarco and his committee for this.

As the palo enters its hole, Zarco and the Caleros retire to a nearby cantina. They discuss strategies for removing Espinosa from the presidency. Someone suggests sending an escrito to the Department of Governance in Mexico City. They also discuss the possibility of Zarco's resigning as head of the church committee.[14] The Caleros take neither action, but the disputing between the Caleros and the Progressives continues to escalate. The Caleros claim in the public voice that Espinosa is capricious and easy to anger.

During the fiesta an article about the padre appears in a Oaxaca City periodical. It claims that he was sent to Villa Alta after being kicked out of his parish in Ocotlán for having sexual relations with young girls of the village. The article also states that the padre is causing trouble in Villa Alta because he has become actively involved in the politics of the village by advising Calero and Negrete. The writer of the article is Amado Amaya, a Villalteco who has been branded a *lépero* (a lowlife) in the public voice because of his loose talk about other villagers.

News of the articles does not reach Villa Alta until after the fiesta, but during the fiesta the role of the padre in the village is a common topic of conversation among Villalteco males. Many who have returned to the village for the fiesta express anger at the padre for forbidding the Friday dance. They argue that he should not become involved in village politics, that he is obstinate and does not respect the people of Villa Alta. In part the financial problems of the church committee derive from the fact that the padre invited five priests from throughout Oaxaca to attend the fiesta and give mass. The committee not only must feed the padre's guests but also pay them 2,000 pesos for each mass. And it appears that the padre has invited his associates, all of them older priests, to deliver a specific message: repeal of article twenty-four of the Mexican Constitution that provides for the separation of church and state.

The fiesta proceeds with successful Thursday and Saturday night dances. The entrepreneur who imported the band from Oaxaca City makes a profit selling bottles of brandy and cola. The band of Villa Alta meets all its obligations, even though it is paid only half its customary fee. At no time during the day or evening are the bands of Villa Alta or Zacatepec without ready bottles of mezcal or aguardiente and cases of warm beer.

After the fiesta, Zarco and Negrete, heads of the fiesta committees, announce to the village that both committees ended the fiesta with a surplus of money—the church committee with 26,000 pesos and the kitchen committee with 35,000 pesos. By claiming a lack of funds, withholding money from the local band, scrimping on some fiesta events, and achieving the cooperation of Villaltecos in paying for and preparing meals for the band of Zacatepec, both committees actually earned healthy sums.[15]

Committee heads may allocate their surpluses either to the Ayuntamiento headed by President Espinosa or to the Catholic church of Villa Alta. Zarco and Negrete claim that Espinosa behaved incorrectly several times during the fiesta preparations and failed to offer assistance to the committees when assistance was needed. Therefore, they give the fiesta surplus to the church for the purchase of more pews.[16]

In early April, President Espinosa calls a meeting of villagers. Even the women attend.[17] Villagers attack Espinosa for both his management of village finances and his conduct during the fiesta. The women, including church leaders, criticize the president for placing several of their husbands in jail for drunkenness during the fiesta. They claim that although getting drunk in public is not acceptable all the time, it is during fiestas.

The case of the padre against the seminarian is also a subject of the junta. Espinosa asks if anyone present has evidence or testimony to present concerning the padre's charges that the seminarian took his money, gun, guitar, and clothes. No one speaks up. Word of the news-paper article critical of the padre has reached Villalteco Progressive voices.

The first showers of the rainy season arrive in April. Before and during the March fiesta the ground was dry and dusty. Smoke from burning fields on the mountainsides filled the air to the north and settled over Villa Alta. As the fiesta season drew to a close the village grew quieter. Visitors returned to Oaxaca City. Once-crowded daily buses arrive in Villa Alta with only three or four passengers. With the first rains minifundistas go to their fields to begin planting maize. At night, the northern skies beyond the village of Camotlán are filled with contin-uous lightning.

The padre's complaint against the seminarian remains in the office of the ministerio público. The women's network has received the infor-mation published by Amaya in the Oaxaca periodical, but it is not discussed openly. Esperanza Blasco and Luisa Zarco continue their efforts to influence the district court judge to intervene in the padre's case. One night in Blasco's kitchen, the judge, after once again hearing the argument that the seminarian stole the padre's possessions, replies, *"No me consta"* ("It is not clear to me"; or, used legally, "I find insuffi-cient evidence"). There is no evidence that the padre possessed the items he claimed were stolen and no evidence that the seminarian stole them. The body of the crime cannot be proven.

The women who support the padre claim that Mendiolea and Es-pinosa are paying the ministerio público not to proceed with the case. They say the ministerio público is waiting for them to offer him money to consign the case to the district court. Luisa Zarco says they will not give him money because they are in the right and for this reason the case will eventually be resolved in the padre's favor.

Now another case, one from outside the district seat, intrudes for a time on the consciousness of Villaltecos. It involves a religious and political dispute in Colonia Reforma, a small village in the marketplace region of the powerful district town of Talea. Six men from the village are brought to the district seat in the custody of their village police and placed in the Villa Alta jail. They have been charged with tearing down the house of a Protestant in their village who refused to contribute toward buying a truck to be owned collectively by the village.

Within two weeks, villagers representing regional assemblies of the smaller villages in the district arrive in Villa Alta aboard a chartered bus. They protest the jailing before the ministerio público, who is examining the case, and the district court judge. From a fund maintained by the regional assemblies, an estimated 5,000 pesos in bail is posted to free the men while they await adjudication of the case.

In the final days of May Luisa Zarco ends her tenure as mayordoma. She enters into the church coffers the unusually large sum of 120,000 pesos. (The usual amount for a mayordoma to enter is about 60,000 pesos.) Luisa has benefited from offerings made during the fiesta and from the contributions of the two fiesta committees. The padre praises Luisa as the best mayordoma and says that he hopes all mayordomas in the future will be as successful.

The two former mayordomas, Esperanza Blasco and the mother of David Mendiolea, receive the padre's praise of Luisa Zarco bitterly. They take his statement as a criticism of past mayordomas and say it was inappropriate for him to give such praise to a woman with Luisa's reputation. Information about Luisa begins to circulate in the public voice. Blasco claims that Luisa is a thief and steals food from her while working in her kitchen. It is claimed that Luisa is having another affair with a bureaucrat. Some Progressives claim they have had affairs with Luisa in exchange for money. The Calero Ezekiel Zarco responds angrily to these tales about his sister.

The most damaging information spread by the elder women is that Luisa and the padre are having an affair. The women claim they saw the padre embracing Luisa on the church grounds. The public voice claims that the padre likes *muchachas*. Discussion begins over whether or not the padre is going to remain in Villa Alta. Word in the voice claims that the padre says he will remain until the Santo Intierro tells him to leave or until his superiors in Oaxaca City send him to another region.

Another article by Amaya appears in a Oaxaca City periodical, repeating his criticism of the padre's behavior. This article, like the one that preceded it, does not become a subject of open discussion in the public voice but is discussed one on one. Some claim that Amaya, like the seminarian, once had a confrontation with the padre in a cantina. After having a few drinks Amaya supposedly said to the padre, "You're not a father, you're only a half-father." Angered, the padre left the cantina but soon returned, accosted Amaya, and began slapping him in the face. Amaya, it is said, left the cantina.

In the middle of May the Escuela Técnica Agropecuaria (ETA), the secondary technical school, loses its teacher of mathematics. None of the teachers are Villaltecos even though the school is located in the district seat, and Villaltecos are critical of the school's staff members because they have changed the focus of the curriculum from agriculture to literacy skills. Now, in conjunction with the Villalteco parents' association connected to the ETA, the school administration intends to appoint Amado Amaya to fill the vacated position. They argue that since Amaya has a university degree certifying him as an *ingeniero* (engineer) he is qualified to teach mathematics. Amaya, the only resident Villalteco with a university degree, is also described by his friends as an expert on Sierra agriculture (he was trained as an agricultural engineer). His coffee fields, the only village fields that are regularly irrigated, yield Villa Alta's highest agricultural profits.

The women of Villa Alta, in discussions that precede Amaya's appointment, express only negative sentiments. They criticize Amaya for his drinking and for being a lépero. Amaya's writing of the two articles against the padre helps solidify their stand against him. Several women claim in private that the articles were unfair and untrue. Their sentiments in favor of the padre appear to grow stronger.

Amaya's appointment generates a wave of protest from the ETA students' association. Many of the protesting students are sons of Villaltecos who support the appointment. The children of active Catholic women from Villa Alta who support the padre are among the strongest of Amaya's opponents. Parents of students from neighboring villages also oppose the appointment. Several of the protesting parents are influential politicians in their villages.

The protests become a frequent topic of discussion in the Villalteco public voice. They are tied to other political problems between Villa Alta and the district villages, within which the ETA has remained a center of controversy. Politicians from district villages opposed the construction of the ETA in the seat in 1973. They also opposed and threatened the then Villalteco mero cacique, Areli Fabela, who claimed responsibility for negotiating the building of the ETA and its siting in the district seat. Later Fabela was slain.

The men who lead the protest against the appointment of Amaya are said to be the same politicians who led the protest against the construction of the ETA. They are political leaders from Betaza, Lachitaa, and Lachirioag, three villages which, both last year and this year, experienced strong political controversies that resulted in much internal divisiveness. Some Villaltecos interpret the opposition to Amaya's appointment as both opposition to Villa Alta and support for the padre.

The two heads of the Villalteco parents' association are the Calero Ezekiel Zarco and Mario Fabela, the brother of the slain cacique. Zarco was one of Areli Fabela's most outspoken opponents and opposed building the ETA. Mario Fabela works in the post office under Zarco's direction. He is a Progressive and opposes the stands of the Caleros, whom he refers to as *negativos*.

Fabela argues an interpretation of his brother's murder that is shared by many Villaltecos even though it was not supported by the findings of the district court investigation in 1974. He claims that leaders from neighboring villages who opposed the ETA conspired to kill his brother. He says they waited for an opportunity to find him alone, and the opportunity arose one Monday evening when the cacique was walking alone in the rain to Temazcalapa, where he taught school. It was on a market day when the "conspirators" were in Villa Alta. Fabela claims they saw his brother leave the village alone and paid a man at the marketplace to follow and kill him.

Now the conspirators are leading the opposition to Amaya's appointment. Fabela and Zarco, though from opposing political groups, support Amaya's appointment, as do all Villalteco men who voice an opinion on the expanding dispute. Fabela's wife, an active Catholic, and son, a student at the ETA, oppose the appointment.

On the street and in the public voice an unusual consensus among Caleros and Progressives arises. President Espinosa and David Mendiolea, who were locked in conflict with Zarco during the fiesta, now join him to lobby the village in support of Amaya. Zarco, a confidant and follower of the padre, is actively supporting one of the padre's most outspoken opponents. And for the first time since before the fiesta, Zarco and Espinosa are speaking to each other.

Zarco and Fabela call a special meeting of the village to discuss the controversy. With some women present the villagers decide to support Amaya's appointment. The women drop their opposition. After this decision, opposition to Amaya from the district village politicians and students appears to increase. Some men in the village begin to speak of a conspiracy to kill Mario Fabela because of his leadership in Amaya's appointment. The men said to be heading the conspiracy are those from Betaza, Lachitaa, and Lachirioag whom some Villaltecos accuse of killing Mario's brother.

While the men and women of Villa Alta have been disputing Amado Amaya's moral worth, disputes between Esperanza Blasco and Luisa Zarco have escalated. Blasco continues to accuse Zarco of stealing food and money from her home. Tito Mendiolea intervenes daily in the disputes. Zarco begins to talk with others about Blasco. She claims that Blasco is losing her memory and misplacing things. She also revives stories about Blasco's past: an illicit affair many years ago and problems with her husband. Blasco says she cannot ask Zarco to leave her home because she is a family member. For the same reason and for fear of retaliation she cannot accuse Zarco of stealing before the president of Villa Alta.

At the same time, Blasco, the mother of David Mendiolea, and several of their friends in the church women's network begin to abandon their support of the padre. Both former mayordomas stop attending mass. Luisa continues to visit the church daily, even though she is no longer mayordoma. Blasco and other men and women in Villa Alta, as well as Villalteco urbanites in Oaxaca City, begin to treat the articles published by Amaya about the padre as information that can be discussed openly.

Toward the end of June, as Villaltecos are drawing together in support of Amaya, women of Progressive families who have been among the strongest supporters of the padre, including Blasco, begin to say that the damaging information about the padre in Amaya's articles is accurate. The padre had indeed been asked to leave Ocotlán because he had relations with young women, they say, and his relationship with Luisa is proof that sexual relations are his downfall. A sentiment expressed by women in the public voice is that both the state and the Catholic church discriminate against Villa Alta. They say that just as bureaucrats are sent to Villa Alta as punishment for infractions (because the seat is so isolated and the district so poor), the padre was sent to Villa Alta as punishment for his behavior in Ocotlán.[18]

The Caleros Benigno and Chucho Blasco discuss the fact that the padre does what he wants to do in spite of the suggestions and requests of Villaltecos. They say he is late for mass and does not keep scheduled appointments. "No one is able to reach the padre," says Chucho. The Caleros recall that one night just prior to the fiesta only a few Villaltecos attended mass. The next day the angry padre forbade the ringing of the church bells to announce mass. The Caleros began to say that the padre is quick to anger and does not try to understand the people of Villa Alta.

The padre's accusations against the seminarian still remain in the office of the ministerio público. And the palo encerado is still standing above the central square. The president insists that the church committee is responsible for removing it, but Zarco argues that the village police are responsible. Zarco and some members of his former committee carry the palo to the church. They ask the padre's permission to store it in a dry place to await the next fiesta of the Santo Intierro. The padre refuses their request and insists that they place the palo in an open field behind the church. They leave it there to rot in the rainy season.

Amaya travels daily to his field on the mountainside of Roayaga, where he is experimenting with maize and some new strains of squash. The old marketplace of Villa Alta has been leveled and jornaleros work daily making cement blocks for a new two-level marketplace. President Espinosa and the police chief supervise the construction. Preparations begin for Villa Alta's September celebration of San Ildefonso.

Esperanza Blasco voices an opinion, now widely shared, that the padre must leave Villa Alta. She says he made two major mistakes. First, he became too involved in the politics of Villa Alta through his frequent consultations in the rectory with Calero, Zarco, and Negrete. Second, he criticized the past mayordomas for not entering more money into the church coffers. He should have realized that the only reason Luisa Zarco entered so much money was because she was able to sell candles during the fiesta.

The third week in June, classes at the ETA end and are followed by graduation ceremonies in the central square of Villa Alta. Some graduating students ask Villaltecos and seconded bureaucrats to be their sponsors at the ceremonies, while others find sponsors from their own villages. Sponsors buy small gifts for the graduating students and share tables at the outdoor ceremonies with them and their families. A dance follows the ceremonies.

Preparations for the dance have been complicated by threats to kill its organizer, Mario Fabela. Fabela refuses to leave his home alone or to walk alone in the village. On market day preceding the ceremonies, a friend of Fabela's from Lachirioag had told him that opposition leaders were laying a trap for him, that they planned to isolate and then kill him. While Fabela was working in the post office, the district village leaders, all of whom were together in Villa Alta for the weekly market, sent word that they wanted to meet with him. Fabela sighted the men from the porch of the post office above the eastern side of the central square. Following a small path that leads away from Ezekiel Zarco's house, Fabela sought refuge in his own home. To members of the dance committee Fabela later explained that he had had a dream about his brother's murder before it occurred. He said that he also had been dreaming about his own assassination and knew his opponents in the district wanted to kill him.

On the night of the graduation ceremonies, the cement court in front of Villa Alta's public school in the central square is filled with dancers, patrons, graduating students, and their families. Mario Fabela stays at home with his wife and children. Villalteco sponsors and the parents of graduating students remain at their tables into the early morning. The Villaltecos and bureaucrats treat the students' parents to brandy and beer sold by the ETA parents' association. Ezekiel Zarco's cousin, the Villalteco telegraph operator who is a vocal Calero and still supports the padre, gets drunk while sharing several bottles of brandy. He walks among the celebrants and says to everyone he passes: "The Truth, the Truth, we have to discuss the Truth." A Progressive dispensing beer and brandy remarks, "All he ever wants to talk about is the truth."

CHAPTER 3

Division in the District Seat

Since 1955, factions of district-seat natives and residents have ruled and disputed in the district seat of Villa Alta. According to Villalteco accounts, many of the disputes that have arisen within the seat have centered on the civic responsibilities of seat residents.

Local activities and development projects created in partnership with external agencies depend on the villagers' voluntary contributions of time, labor, and economic resources. Voluntarism is the foundation of village civil law. The villager who does not fulfill his duties may be fined or jailed at the discretion of committee heads and the village president. Voluntarism is realized through the *cargo* (burden or charge) system, the voluntary associations and committees, and the village authority structure. It is also realized through Catholic church committees and lay positions.

The cargo system exists side by side with political bossism (*caciquismo*) as means by which Villalteco males achieve prestige and power. Caciquismo predominates in Villa Alta; the cargo system legitimizes political boss rule. Caciquismo has captured the historical and political imaginations of Villaltecos, while rules of the cargo system provide villagers a way to voice their complaints against cacique lieutenants and supporters who hold "elected" positions in the village government.

Some Villalteco caciques moved into their positions by successfully developing village projects while holding the elected office of president. Others, such as David Mendiolea and Juan Calero, never served as village president. No Villalteco campesinos or jornaleros have become caciques through service in the presidency. Only schoolteachers, government employees, and merchants are candidates for cacique status.

The civil-religious hierarchy has been the focus of most village studies in Mexico (for an excellent review see Greenberg 1981). But no Villalteco has achieved power through the *mayordomía*—the sponsorship of religious festivals and service in caretaker positions of the Catholic church. Some Villalteco males have substituted voluntary service to the church for more demanding civil duties. Individual males are expected to sponsor specific fiesta events, such as a lunch or dinner for a visiting band or a fireworks display. These duties, however, are now being assumed by urban committees and caciques (for a further example of urban participation in village fiesta economies see Crumrine 1969). The political division of Villa Alta has multiplied the number of village leaders who at times compete for power through contributions to local ceremonies.

The cargo system is a focus of controversy between village political parties, for voluntary service in its positions has required farm workers to leave the fields and employees to leave wage-paying jobs.[1] Employees have been more successful in combining their jobs with municipal service, since village offices are near their own offices and the school; all are located on the central square. Under cacique rule, serving a three-year term in a municipal office is not demanding, for essentially it is the village president and the caciques who broker village projects with state and federal governments and sit in counsel to reach important local decisions. Often the president also fills the roles of *síndico* (prosecutor) and *alcalde* (judge) in the village court.

The secular cargo system is age-graded. It involves progressive movement of individuals through the positions of *topil* (messenger), *policía* (police), *regidor* (head of the police force), *regidor encargado de las llaves* (the person responsible for the district jail and those confined in it), síndico, alcalde, secretario, and presidente.[2] In a traditional cargo system, authority in village affairs increases with age, length of voluntary service, movement up the service ladder, and satisfactory fulfillment of duties. In Villa Alta the position of president precedes that of alcalde along the cargo ladder.

Serving on committees is another important aspect of local community obligation. Committees are formed for the upkeep of municipal and religious buildings, to run fiestas, and for school administration. Other committees deal with developmental issues, such as governmental assistance to agriculture, the CONASUPO, and village roads. Playing in the village band precludes service on fiesta committees. Committees other than those for fiestas generally meet at night, so they do not entail financial hardship.

The most demanding positions in Villa Alta are president, regidor, regidor encargado de las llaves, and police (reserved for young men entering village service). Government grants to pay workers on new construction projects have removed much of the financial hardship for these jobs, for the police and the regidores also serve as construction crew members and are paid on an hourly basis. In reality, the cargo system rechannels funds from employees to jornaleros. Villaltecos who do not wish to serve their cargo pay for *suplentes* (substitutes) or are fined suplente wages by the village government. Many employees opt for payment instead of service. Fiesta committees also provide opportunities for jornaleros when employees pay not to meet the daily obligations of fiesta preparations.

The obligation of cargo service in Villa Alta has become a form of governmental employment that maintains a paid work force for the undertaking of community development projects. The Caleros, who generally oppose such development and the expansion of local service obligations, are opposed to this economic upscaling of the cargo system. Some analyses of the economic and social functions of cargo systems have found them a conservative force in village development, for they redirect local surplus into community maintenance and religious ceremonies and away from larger capitalist markets (Wolf 1955, Nash, M. 1958).

Dow (1974b, p. 23) argued that the peasant community's civil-religious organization "stimulates the production of surplus for ceremonial exchange and then redistributes it effectively within the local group without making it available to the dominant class." The stratification of Villa Alta and the local economic roles of urban villagers are rendering the Villalteco cargo system a source of local municipal development and security for minifundistas who supplement their incomes by working as day laborers. The cargo system and, to a lesser degree, the fiesta system redirect surplus downward from the families of employees and merchants directly into the hands of jornaleros and minifundistas.

This redirection occurs within a highly stratified system that ranges from urban wealth and large-scale cash-cropping to subsistence agriculture. Villalteco participation in both the larger capitalist markets and the state bureaucratic sector provides local stratification with enough wealth at the top to produce surplus that flows into the community and the state and national marketplaces. As Cancian (1965,

1967) argued, demands for wealth in the civil-religious hierarchy do not increase proportionately with local development of surplus through participation in capitalist markets.

As Villaltecos pay for rather than work in the cargo system, they contribute to the making of jornaleros and minifundistas as a lower service class without the political power of higher cargo positions. Local stratification and urban villager participation in fiesta economies relieves some of the pressure of cargo obligations from villagers with smaller and less dependable incomes. But it also relieves them of a political forum. As a counterforce, historical increases in the salaried population of Villa Alta have freed more villagers for voluntary— though not cargo-based—participation in village politics. That, in turn, has helped support the formation of two local political groups, each with different sets of local and urban leadership. Greater local political centralization compensates somewhat for the loss of campesino power in the cargo system, for Caleros and Progressives now vie for their shifting support.

The pressure that campesinos can put on latifundistas is increasing in another way. The changing role of the cargo system, resulting from increased state participation in the local economy along with the presence of a government-subsidized CONASUPO, is creating strains in the local cash-crop economy. Labor for the picking of coffee beans is now scarce in Villa Alta, for jornaleros say they can earn enough money in three days working for the village government to buy a week's worth of maize and beans in the CONASUPO. Jornaleros who support Caleros can withhold their labor from Progressive latifundistas and their supporters. As a result, Villalteco landholders have come to rely more and more on the reluctant labor force in neighboring Zapotec villages.[3]

Villaltecos relate the history of their village in terms of individual figures, their actions, and the opponents of their actions. Thus they glorify caciquismo in historical tales. The Vallalteco version of how the village has developed, which expresses a viewpoint common in Zapotec and Mixe villages, contrasts with analyses of peasant villages that locate the forces of conservatism and change in village civil-religious hierarchies and the village's marginal participation in national and international capitalist marketplaces. The local view of power is less deterministic and more individualistic.

Local versions of the history of Sierra villages in the twentieth century emphasize conflicts and the roles of individuals in their resolution. They follow a common theme that pits a political leader, usually a cacique, against his antagonists. Historical tales vary with the purpose of relating them. A popular romantic theme attributes to leaders and their challengers special, and at times, superhuman abilities. Villagers have preserved and romanticized their pasts in the memory of personalities like Areli Fabela who symbolize historical conflicts between villages and families. As symbols, individuals and their families represent various modes of conflict resolution.

The idea that an individual leader and broker may accumulate power that dominates village conflicts and extends into the Sierra is not confined to Villaltecos who trace their descent to Spanish *conquistadores*. Favored tales of caciquismo in Villa Alta relate the exploits of Luis Rodriguez of Zacatepec, the most powerful Mixe leader from the middle 1930s until his death in 1959. (For various Sierra tales about Rodriguez and caciquismo see Laviada 1978.) Some residents of Zacatepec considered Rodriguez a reincarnation of the Mixe king Condoy. Some Villaltecos, like their Mixe neighbors, say Rodriguez was able to will his own invisibility. Most attribute his power to brokerage and the backing of political leaders in Oaxaca City and Mexico City. One component of the Rodriguez legend is that he resolved a three-year conflict between Villa Alta and its neighbor Lachirioag that arose in the middle 1950s over the location of the weekly marketplace. As the story goes, Rodriguez threatened to intervene with armed soldiers gathered from his backers in the Zacatepec district. But other Villaltecos say that Manuel Orozco, a cacique and acting judge of the district court, resolved the conflict through personal charisma and the threat of armed intervention by the Oaxacan state.

Villalteco political conflicts over the past thirty years thus can be seen as falling into four major periods depending on which caciques were most powerful: rule by the Torres triumvirate (pre-1955); rule by the Mendiolea triumvirate (1955–74); village political division with Calero-Torres rule (1975–80); and village political division with Mendiolea rule (since 1981).

Prior to 1955, the seat's most powerful men were teachers and employees in state district offices. The mero cacique was Raul Torres. His ruling triumvirate included David Sesto, a teacher, and Manuel Amaya, who was the district court judge. Native Villaltecos ran district offices and exercised wide discretion in their roles as tax collectors, judges, and prosecutors. Amaya and the district prosecutor usually heard cases in their homes rather than in their offices, and many cases were not recorded on court dockets. Zapotec villagers preferred this personal touch to state law (though not to village law); their use of Villalteco judgment declined with later professionalization of the district court. Through fees charged for services, Villalteco office heads increased their personal wealth and landholdings. They were the village's wealthiest and most powerful patrons, the foundation of their political power lying in their exercise of discretion in the management of state district bureaucracies.

In the middle 1950s the state ended its practice of bestowing control of district offices on local politicians and began a policy of rotating bureaucrats from throughout Oaxaca. Trade and credit became the major sources of local power as Villa Alta's marketplace grew and Lachirioag's and Camotlán's declined. Young merchants and teachers replaced the bureaucrats as village leaders.

David Mendiolea, the new Progressive mero cacique, ran his father's dry-goods store on the central square. He built the store into a larger enterprise by selling musical instruments to Mixe and Zapotec villagers. He also became the major middleman for cultivators of coffee in the region and extended credit and made loans to district campesinos. The caciques who allied with Mendiolea during his twenty-year rule were Areli Fabela and Benjamin Blasco. Fabela was a teacher who walked each school day to his post in the northern village of Temazcalapa, an hour and a half from Villa Alta. He attained cacique status through the personal ties to state politicians and federal bureaucrats that he developed while he was president of Villa Alta. Blasco, who also served as president, derived his power from wealth and his movement through the cargo system. He owned land, baked and sold bread, and was a moneylender. This latter function made him, along with Mendiolea, one of Villa Alta's most powerful patrons.

For twenty years the caciques and village presidents used their roles as brokers between the village and the external world to nurture personal contacts with politicians and bureaucrats within state and national administrations. Through the presidency, less wealthy, salaried employees developed personal power and local respect through village projects partially funded by state and national agencies. The major theme of Mendiolea's rule was voluntary participation by villagers in the development of the district seat. Mendiolea also attempted to exclude Catholic church officials from village politics.

Mendiolea's triumvirate brought electricity and potable water to Villa Alta. They refurbished the crumbling Catholic church and built a secondary school. Their last and most controversial project was the construction in 1974 of the Escuela Técnica Agropecuaria (ETA). Much of the construction of the ETA was accomplished with the voluntary labor of seat residents. At the same time a one-lane dirt road that ran between Yalálag and Oaxaca City was extended to Villa Alta.

After Torres lost power to Mendiolea he did not withdraw from local politics. He was the ideological leader of a small but vocal conservative faction of Villaltecos, who opposed the Mendiolea projects. The Torres faction argued that many Villaltecos were too poor to leave their fields to work on projects for which they were not compensated. The faction also called for a larger role for the Catholic church in local governance. At that time only poor campesinos without influence served as the church's mayordomo. Torres's faction joined with neighboring district villagers to oppose the construction of the technical school.

Mendiolea, Fabela, and Blasco became the targets of frequent verbal attacks and threats by those who opposed their projects. The most direct threats were made through *anónimos*—mimeographed messages that threatened the lives of Progressive leaders. Fabela, especially, was attacked for what he considered his major accomplishment, the building of the ETA. One message warned Fabela:

> I treat you like my son-in-law.
> I will plant you in a grave
> And give you a ticket to Hell.

Deeper currents were eroding Mendiolea's power. In 1973, after a state office of the Comisión del Compra de Café was established in Villa Alta, all Villalteco farmers and those of the region were to sell their coffee to it rather than to private middlemen like Mendiolea. That removed a major source of Mendiolea's patronage. Also, Torres's four sons, all but one of whom were lawyers in Oaxaca City and Mexico City, developed important personal contacts in state and national politics and governance. Other Villalteco urbanites also were active in village politics, and many were supporters of Torres. Torres's sons were joined in their political activism by the offspring of Sesto and Amaya, Torres's old allies. They, too, gained wealth and power through their acquisition of land and their rise in urban and state bureaucracies.

Torres was supported locally by the teachers Juan Calero and Alberto and Tino Negrete. Ezekiel Zarco, a Villalteco government employee whose mentor was Sesto, the former cacique, joined the teachers to form the core of the faction. Some campesino leaders also joined them. Many villagers said Torres and his lieutenants were responsible for the anónimos.

In 1974, President Blasco sometimes called at least one *tequío* (village work project) a week for work on the technical school, and some weeks three. Campesinos and some employees worked all day in the heat of the dry season, breaking away portions of the steep mountainside with shovels and picks, carrying bricks, and clearing land with machetes. Citizens of other villages in the district were supposed to call their own tequíos and travel to Villa Alta to help, but none came. Many residents of these outlying villages said the school would benefit only the Villaltecos. The Torres and Calero Conservatives argued prophetically that the school would bring greater economic benefit to Villa Alta's closest neighbor, Lachirioag, than to the seat. These Conservatives, however, were a small faction, without enough support to weaken the strength of the caciques.

On a March evening in 1974 Fabela was murdered. He had left Villa Alta to walk to Temazcalapa. Traveling alone, he had taken refuge from an unusual rainfall in a small hut along a path about thirty minutes below the central square. When his dogs returned the next morning without him his family rushed to the path. They found his body, marked by the slashes of a machete, lying on the dirt floor of the hut.

Fabela's parents testified before the district court secretary that the Conservative opponents of the caciques had killed him. Fabela had passed the homes of campesinos who were allied with the Conservatives and was killed in the ranchito of the Conservative Celestino Jimenez, a large landholder who held a personal grudge against Fabela. President Blasco passed information on Conservatives to the district court judge, who formulated accusations against them. The judge requested that judicial police from Oaxaca City come to Villa Alta to apprehend the presumed assassins and jail them in the state capital.

The night the police arrived Blasco warned Torres, Calero, the Negretes, and Zarco to take refuge. But Jimenez and the accused campesino Conservatives were not warned. The judicial police apprehended them, bound their hands with rope, and led them out of Villa Alta. Eventually, they were found innocent. The murderer was identified as a man from Camotlán who supposedly had also sought refuge from the rain in the hut and had been threatened and insulted by Fabela. The offended man left, but returned to kill the sleeping Fabela. One of his companions that night, who told the story, was apprehended by Villaltecos and placed in the district jail, but later escaped. The murderer was never apprehended.

As Villaltecos identified outsiders as the murderers they also grew concerned about political offenders in the case. The Progressives had violated the village ethic by calling in state force. President Blasco had defended men of his own social standing—even his political opponents—and had used campesinos as scapegoats. Blasco and the Fabela family had disrupted the balance of social and political relations in Villa Alta.

The growing political division affected social life. Villaltecos began to fear that the political conflicts would escalate into open violence. Stricter rules on public drinking and public confrontations were enforced. Villagers curtailed informal socializing in public places after dark.

In January 1975, the elder Torres was elected president of the village. But Torres, weakened by age and alcohol, was only the titular leader for a new majority group headed by Juan Calero. A native Villalteco schoolteacher who was young, articulate, and energetic, Calero was not an important village patron. His power lay in the support of three groups: members of the Torres faction; some influential Villalteco urban professionals and bureaucrats; and the growing population of immigrants from outlying villages.

The new coalition of conservatives and campesinos was joined in control of the village by urbanites, including the sons of Torres and Sesto and the brothers of Calero. These urbanites founded the Villalteco Cultural Association as a Oaxaca City political group supporting Calero. Torres was back in power, and so were his family and friends.

The foundations of local power shifted once again from economic to political brokerage, with the most powerful man in Villa Alta standing at the nexus of interconnected networks of bureaucrats, politicians, and local campesinos. As a result of their diversity, the ideology of the Caleros was inconsistent and vague, unlike that of Mendiolea. Among the supporters of Calero were both supporters and opponents of regional assemblies, "Spanish" descendants who were salaried employees, and some persons who called for the relinquishing of Villa Alta's seat status. Nevertheless, two aspects of Calero ideology were clear: the Caleros consistently supported diminished roles in local governance for voluntarism, lower village quotas, and greater participation of Catholic officials in establishing village policies.

In giving the church greater authority the Caleros actually were attempting to bolster their own authority by emphasizing the importance of morality. The access of younger Caleros to legal and moral privileges was limited; by moving the context of local evaluations to a more strictly religious realm, they saw a chance to gain more privileges than the less openly devout Progressives. Occasional Calero arguments about "the Truth" could be interpreted in this light. Most Calero lieutenants volunteered service to the church without protest.

When the Caleros assumed power, Villa Alta's immigrants had become a pivotal population in the competition for local authority. The political choices and alliances of recent immigrants, unlike those of native Villaltecos, were not influenced by kinship or past conflicts and disputes. Patronage tied them more weakly to specific political figures. As farmers, their allegiances were not influenced by office ties and managers. A shortage of day laborers in the district seat had increased competition among large landholders for the help of immigrants in picking coffee.

Mendiolea now moved his political and economic base to Oaxaca City. He became a leader in exile and focused his energy on the expansion of his urban retail business. In the process he continued to expand his personal political ties.

President Torres rarely appeared in the Ayuntamiento office. He soon stepped down, and Calero placed three other men in the presidency in quick succession. One, a campesino who held little land, was a native of Lachirioag. Another was a native of Villa Alta who raised sheep. The third was Damien Amaya, a son of Manuel Amaya, the former member of the Torres triumvirate. Calero removed all of them before they completed their three-year terms. None gained personal power in Villa Alta as a result of the presidency.

The major accomplishment of the Caleros was the building of a new road connecting Villa Alta with the state capital. The road built by the Mendiolea triumvirate was frequently impassable. The new one-lane dirt road, federally funded and maintained, ran through the district of Zacatepec; unlike the older road it passed through few of the Villa Alta district villages that opposed the seat and its residents. The Villalteco Cultural Association in Oaxaca City published a book that chronicled the Caleros' role in the construction of the new road. It included copies of their correspondence with state and federal officials.[4]

The Calero response to villagers who defied them was inconsistent with the political group's opposition to state involvement in village affairs. Calero and the sons of Torres used their state government contacts to get judicial officials to cooperate in the jailing of Villalteco campesinos, merchants, political leaders, and employees who refused to comply with Calero's demands. Like the Progressives before them the Caleros drew too heavily on the political and legal resources of the state in their attempts to rule the residents of Villa Alta—a violation of the ethic of local control.

Among those whom Calero jailed was Benjamin Blasco, the former cacique who, though widely criticized as a Progressive leader, was also a respected elder and patron in several Villalteco families. When Damien Amaya was being entered into the presidency in a traditional New Year's Eve ceremony—the most valued secular ritual in Villa Alta—Blasco shorted the village's electricity. The residents of Villa Alta and urbanites who gathered in the central square were thrown into darkness, and some feared there might be violence. Blasco's act had been witnessed; he was jailed, then released under a demand of *amparo* (protection by the state judiciary from actions by judicial officials).[5]

By the late 1970s Calero's support had begun to erode. Then the governorship of Oaxaca changed hands and the Caleros lost their influence over the state judicial system. In 1980, Manuel Gil, a supporter of Mendiolea and head of the Villa Alta secondary school, became president of Villa Alta. Mendiolea and Blasco returned to power, and the Caleros became the opposition group.

Gil and Mendiolea used the federal government's policy of decentralization to direct funds now provided to Villa Alta (eight million pesos annually), as well as additional support from state and federal agencies, to construct a new *municipio* (municipal building) and offices for several state and federal agencies in the district seat.[6] The completion of the municipal building, strongly opposed by the Caleros, signaled Gil's rise to cacique status. But Mendiolea's increased wealth (from his urban business interests) and his political status in Oaxaca City placed him above both Gil and Blasco as the primary force behind the development of Villa Alta.[7] Mendiolea spoke of frequent visits to the office of Oaxaca's governor; at the same time, he cautiously criticized some policies of the ruling national political party, PRI (Institutional Revolutionary Party).[8]

As centralized agencies increased their outlay of funds to Villa Alta, the seat's isolation in the district increased. Regional assemblies and Protestant churches brought organization and new alliances among outlying villagers who opposed both the state and the district seat. How to deal with what Villaltecos viewed as growing threats in the region became a major issue of debate between the Caleros and the supporters of Mendiolea.[9] The power of both groups was tenuous, for it was based on the shifting alliances of a growing number of immigrants and personal ties to politicians and bureaucrats of the external world of fluctuating factional power and politics.

In 1983, Gil was succeeded as president by Otilio Espinosa, a Villalteco schoolteacher and former Calero who had switched his allegiance to Mendiolea after the Caleros lost power. Some Progressives said Espinosa was *sucio*—dirtied by the fact that he had not been a supporter of Mendiolea during troubled times. Espinosa initiated a project with state and federal funds and the cooperation of Progressive caciques to build a new market in the central square. He was to direct its construction in Villa Alta while Mendiolea provided communication and negotiation with government agencies in the capital. Like the municipio, the marketplace project would provide jobs for day laborers. Control of federal decentralization funds could be allocated by Espinosa to pay villagers who worked on the projects that Mendiolea brokered.

In early 1984, the caciques still held power but the Caleros were actively generating support for the removal of Espinosa. His good points and his bad points were bandied about in the public voice, but no accusations of corruption had arisen. Espinosa, Torres, Zarco, and the Negretes remained the core of the Calero group.

Mendiolea traveled from Oaxaca City to Villa Alta at least twice a month for two or three days. In addition to giving direction to Espinosa and consulting with Gil and Blasco, Mendiolea managed the village's finances. The district judge claimed allegiance with Mendiolea; however, he also said he would ally with whomever was in power.

Yet Calero power was continuing to increase, and the political groups of the divided district seat were locked as more or less equal opponents in dispute over principles of governance and the nature of village boundaries to the external world. It is in this atmosphere of group-based political conflict and perceived disorder and threats from the external world that the disputes of 1984 developed and expanded.

The decade preceding 1984 was, therefore, one of important changes in the lives of many villages in the district of Villa Alta. At the beginning of the decade, the murder of Fabela, one of the district's most influential political figures, increased tensions between the district seat and its neighbors. These tensions persisted into 1984 as some Villaltecos continued to find conspiracies against the seat by the agricultural villagers. In the region, factions and villages formed political confederations, and Protestant conversions and churches increased in number. First, the promise of economic boom and then the reality of economic crisis in the Mexican economy appeared to fuel local perceptions that the world outside the village was disorderly and unpredictable.[10]

Changes in the external world were matched by changes in the district seat. In 1981, the mayordomía of the Catholic church was turned over to the women of the village. Men were no longer willing to care for church property on a daily basis or to make and sell candles without financial compensation.[11] The female leaders of the church and the first mayordomas were members of nuclear families of both Calero and Mendiolea leaders. In contrast, most active Catholic men were Calero lieutenants. During her tenure, the work of the mayordoma was a major source of local income for the church, and she was responsible for sacred church objects. Any loss of funds or property during her tenure led to gossip, if not to accusations concerning her possible participation in theft.

Another change was brought about by the stepped-up migration of the 1970s and early 1980s, which had two effects on the population of the extended district seat: it increased the incidence of exogamy and increased the percentage of nonnatives in the resident village population. Unlike their parents, many of the young Villalteco men and women who married in the decade preceding 1984 did not establish ties that cut across the political oppositions of their elders. Kinship accounts indicate that there was very little intermarriage among the nuclear families of Villa Alta's most powerful political opponents. The nuclear families of the Torres triumvirate intermarried, but they did not exchange spouses with the Mendiolea triumvirate. There was intermarriage, however, among the families who were the supporters of the most powerful Villalteco leaders. Although the leaders were divided by kinship, their followers were not. Ties of kinship and patronage overlapped with those of political allegiance to caciques, but ties of *compadrazgo* (ritual godparenthood) and kinship also tied members of one faction to those of another.

Marital choices of native Villaltecos were also influenced by a largely unstated status system that recognized distinctions among families on the basis of occupation and descent. The sons and daughters of native Villalteco bureaucrats, merchants, and latifundistas were encouraged to marry each other and discouraged from marrying the natives of other district villages. Acceptable exceptions were descendants of Villaltecos who had migrated to or from such villages as Betaza, Reagúi and Camotlán. These covert status-based rules of marriage mitigated against the intermarrying of immigrants to the district seat and native Villaltecos.

Increased exogamy among native Villaltecos, the growth and maturation of the immigrant populations of the 1950s, and the arrival of new immigrants to the seat in the 1970s generated two types of local social distance. Kin ties that had facilitated social exchange among the families of followers of opposed politicians weakened, and the population of village residents not tied by kinship to politically powerful Villalteco families increased.

Alliances to Villalteco political leaders among the immigrant families of the seat were, therefore, different from alliances among the leaders and their families. First, immigrant alliances were stronger when they were to a particular leader, for they were not mitigated by kinship ties to their opponents or throughout the village in general. Second, immigrant alliances were more shifting. They moved as intense loyalty from one leader to another, for they did not overlap with kinship ties and were not based in historical alliances across generations. Both of these factors, along with changes in Villalteco marriage patterns, contributed to the spread of factionalism into political dualism and the intensity of the struggle among Villalteco political leaders for the support and loyalty of villagers.[12]

Distancing forces facilitated the continuation of the village division initiated by Torres's return to power in 1975. Coupled with the weak-

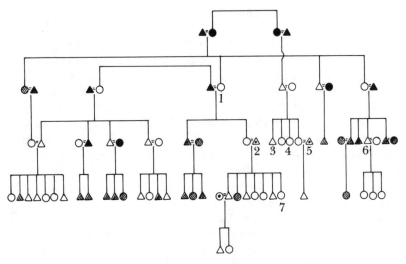

Figure 1. The Blasco-Vera Compound, 1974.

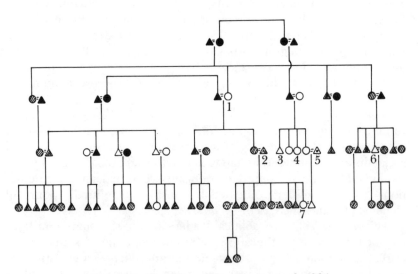

Figure 2. The Blasco-Vera Compound, 1984.

△ Man   ■ Deceased   1. Esperanza Blasco
○ Woman   ◉ Not native of Villa Alta   2. Urbano Estrada
                  ▨ Not resident of Villa Alta 3. Ezekiel Zarco
                  = Marriage   4. Luisa Zarco
                                                5. Alberto Madero
                                                6. Tito Mendiolea
                                                7. Rosalinda Estrada

ened political role of local patronage, the absence of kin obligations contributed to reducing the population of Villaltecos obliged to support specific political leaders. Also reduced was the population of those persons who were neutral or inactive in intergenerational battles as the result of active kin ties to two or more opposed local politicians and patrons.

The native Villalteco Vera/Blasco family is a good example of the effects of increased urban migration. Figure 1 contains one strain of the Blasco family and some members of the Vera family. All members of each family were residents of, or frequent visitors to, a family compound composed of six houses. Exceptions were the Zarco family, kin of Esperanza Blasco. Figure 2 shows kin of the same family in 1984. Two-thirds of the family members on the chart who were alive in 1974 were residents of Villa Alta, while only one-fourth of the living members were Villa Alta residents in 1984. Whereas in the 1930s to 1950s the pattern was for at least one son of a Villalteco to remain to live in Villa Alta, in the 1970s and 1980s the one son, in some families, was not remaining behind. Four houses that the Blasco and Vera families had filled in 1974 were rented to state employees or migrants in 1984.

A household composition census I conducted in 1984 demonstrated that most Villaltecos who remained in Villa Alta married natives of Villa Alta. The few exceptions were marriages between Villaltecos and natives of district Zapotec villages. Only twenty-six percent of native Villalteco residents in Villa Alta married outside their village.

The role intermarriage could play as a counterbalance to the factors that generated social distance between Villa Alta's populations, factions, and groups is shown by a union in the Vera/Blasco family that took place in 1984. The marriage tied the families of two political opponents, one an important lieutenant of Mendiolea and the other an equally important lieutenant of Calero. The backgrounds of Calero and his lieutenants, with the exception of Torres and his sons, were quite different from those of the most powerful supporters of Mendiolea. Although most of the differences between the two groups were based on political and religious issues, one social difference they perceived as a factor that distinguished their local identities was stated at the *pedida* (the occasion) at which the groom asked the father of the bride for permission to marry his daughter.

Urbano Estrada, the father of the bride, Rosalinda, was one of Mendiolea's strongest supporters, as were his wife, sons, and other daughters. Estrada and his sons defined their social relations on the basis of politics. They had cut their social ties to members of the Calero group, and in 1984 they refused to talk to some people who had been their friends ten years earlier. Alberto Madero, the father of the groom, was a major supporter of Calero and had served as one of Calero's village presidents during the 1970s. His wife was the sister of Ezekiel Zarco, one of the leaders of the Calero group.

Estrada and his wife opposed the marriage. Madero and his wife were in favor of it. The patrons, who had been invited to participate in the pedida to give advice to the couple as well as to consent to their betrothal, were Mendiolea and Zarco. All gathered one afternoon at Estrada's home. Mendiolea's mother and Estrada's mother-in-law, Esperanza Blasco, who was also an aunt of the groom's mother and uncle, were invited as witnesses and peacekeepers. Estrada explained before the pedida that he would have to give his consent to the marriage even though he opposed it. He said that his daughter and the young man had spent time together alone.

The session lasted about an hour and a half, during which each patron offered advice on marital relations. The point Zarco stressed repeatedly was that the bride and groom were of different social levels. That, he said, was their greatest problem. The fathers of the young man and woman had both been born in Zapotec villages. Both had married women of Villa Alta, then moved to their wives' villages. But Estrada was a schoolteacher and his adult sons and daughters were all telegraph operators. Madero was a campesino who operated a small stand selling vegetables, beer, and eggs in the weekly marketplace. His son had no occupation but was expected to be a farmer like his father. Estrada's wife was a descendant of the Veras, considered by Villaltecos a Spanish family line. Madero's wife was a Zarco, Villa Alta's largest family but not infused with Spanish blood.

The pedida points to distinctions not often voiced but clearly recognized in Villalteco social relations. Such distinctions stratified the village on the basis of status defined by wealth and descent. Economic stratification was a point of contention in the political battles between the Caleros and the Progressives.

Events that followed the marriage suggest, however, that rights and duties established in relations between families of the bride and groom assumed precedence over the social and political division of the village as the foundation of relationships between the two families. Prior to the marriage, the families interrelated primarily through avoidance. The parents of the bride and her brothers and sisters had moved to Oaxaca City, and the groom's parents, some aunts, an uncle, and a grandparent lived in Villa Alta. Visits by the groom or members of his family to Oaxaca City and visits by members of the bride's family to Villa Alta were not marked by visits across families except through formally arranged discussions of matters related to the wedding. The bride lived with her grandmother, Esperanza Blasco, in Villa Alta. The groom's mother and her family, including her brother Ezekiel Zarco and her three sisters, referred to Blasco as an aunt (see Figure 2).[13] Blasco and the groom's family, especially his mother and brothers and sisters, were all active in the Catholic church and saw each other there frequently. Since the groom's family had a small booth in the Villa Alta marketplace, they traveled from their home near the top of the village to the central square, near Blasco's home, at least once a week. The father of the groom played in the Villa Alta band, so he often traveled to the central square for band practice. Nevertheless, prior to the marriage there was no informal visiting or sharing between the two families.

Following the marriage, patterns of visiting and exchange developed. The bride's father, when he visited Villa Alta, ate at least one meal in the home of the groom's family. The groom's mother and father began visiting regularly with Blasco. The groom's father, when he traveled to Oaxaca City, stayed at the home of the bride's parents, as did the groom's aunts. Favors, such as buying goods in Oaxaca City and Mexico City for members of each others' families, were exchanged as an unquestioned obligation. The father of the bride agreed to rent a room near the central square to the groom's father as a new location for his business. Luisa Zarco, a sister of the groom's mother, began working in Esperanza Blasco's kitchen. On market days the groom ate in Blasco's kitchen, and his parents always stopped in to visit and chat.

The bride's family entered into the new associations reluctantly. At times the new reciprocity caused tension and economic hardship. But the Villaltecos viewed the exchanges as obligations that could not be shirked. The bride's father, though he participated in the new visiting patterns and exchanges, bemoaned all, stating that he would rather not see or spend time with the family of the groom. We have already seen in chapter 2 how relations developed between Luisa Zarco and Esperanza Blasco.

Intermarriage obligated the sharing of economic resources, opportunities, social aid, and social activities across families. Through intermarriage, interfamilial visiting patterns were initiated. Intermarriage provided a source of social cohesion as it cut across politically opposed families and weakened the effect on the larger Villalteco population of intergenerational conflicts between the triumvirates of Mendiolea and Torres and their families.

Kinship thus was not a certain predictor of political alliance or stance. In two powerful Villalteco families, brothers took opposite sides in the political division and their nuclear families did not socialize even though, in one of the families, the brothers were next-door neighbors and residents of a larger family compound. But most nuclear families shared political allegiances, ideologies, and enemies, and marriage across families offered an acceptable rationale for establishing reciprocal relations even with one's political opponents.

Another change came in the 1980s as urbanites assumed a more organized and active role in village politics. They attempted to exercise power in the seat through their personal ties to state politicians, bureaucrats, and religious leaders.

The urban Caleros were opposed in Oaxaca City and Mexico City by a younger and more loosely organized coalition of Villaltecos—the offspring of Mendiolea's supporters and contemporaries. Most of Mendiolea's young urban supporters were, like their parents, teachers and telegraph operators. The Spanish-speaking Villaltecos had provided the majority of teachers for the primary schools of villages in the seat's marketplace region. From teaching positions in their own region, many Villaltecos had transferred to schools nearer Oaxaca City. Other Villaltecos then filled their positions in the Sierra. Also, Villa Alta hosted a regional telegraph office. There young Villaltecos apprenticed for employment in urban telegraph offices. In 1974, no fewer than twenty-seven Villaltecos worked in Mexico City's Centro de Telégrafos.

Young Villalteco employees played important financial roles in their extended families. They provided funds for their parents to apply toward the education of younger children. Their financial contributions were also important in village-based competition for status. Though the offspring of Mendiolea's traditional supporters were poorer than many urban Caleros, they formed an important component of the mero cacique's political foundation. They raised funds among urban Villaltecos and paid personal quotas as contributions to development projects that were the theme of Mendiolea rule. Mendiolea championed the young urbanites as examples of responsible villagers.

The expansion and pluralization of the district seat contributed to local concern about village boundaries and authority as Villaltecos perceived mounting threats to local control from the growing regional movements.[14] But, as the disputes recounted in chapter 2 illustrate, increased pluralization of the seat population also provided important organizational resources in the use of village law to assert local control.

CHAPTER 4

The Anatomy of a Dispute

Hoebel characterized a conflict as a crucible in which a society's tensions shine most clearly (1954). Conflict evolves into disputing, and a dispute expresses and tests the relationships of the disputants to authority, social process, and law. A dispute is a public hearing that calls for public evaluation and public choice. And the cumulative choices made by the disputants help determine the way law develops.

Certainly, the disputes in the district seat of Villa Alta in 1984 both expressed and tested relationships among the groups that were vying for authority. These disputes, developing out of the interpersonal conflicts of a few villagers, eventually placed in confrontation the leaders of Villa Alta's two political groups, the Caleros and the Progressives. They involved the governing Ayuntamiento of Villa Alta and its president, the region's Catholic priest and the women of Villa Alta's Catholic church network, the state district prosecutor and judge, urbanites from Oaxaca City and Mexico City, and the Zapotec residents of outlying villages.

As the disputes developed they spawned arguments, gossip, and family discussions. Villaltecos saw their neighbors and kin, friends and opponents from the viewpoint of local rights and duties. Players in the disputes became the symbols of pressing issues in the conflict over local governance: Should the Catholic church have a greater voice? Should nonnative residents who had moved from neighboring villages play larger roles? Should villagers be held to the traditional process of

[57]

village maintenance—the payment of quotas and voluntary time—even in hard times? Should political bosses continue to rule? Events then moved the disputes to a new level as local perceptions of a threatening external world were given concrete expression by outsiders who came into Villa Alta and became a part of the disputes.

Villaltecos did not take their disputes into any well-structured, specifically legal forums clearly delineated in time and space. Instead, they turned the day-to-day life of the village into an open stage on which everyone could dispute and debate and gossip, and all could act as *auteurs* of the denouement of the disputes.

I was present for many of the exchanges, although, since the disputes were villagewide, there were certainly many dispute-related events and relationships of which I was not aware. However, I did attempt to follow the disputes by frequently touching base with the major actors or their allies. I also frequently checked information about developing disputes with my regular informants in interview sessions. Two informants became invaluable to my research. One was a village leader, though not a boss, who was one of the few Villaltecos not actively involved in the village's partisan politics. With him I was able to discuss my research openly and to evaluate it. The other informant was the woman who had prepared my meals ten years earlier and was a senior member of the family with whom I had lived. Almost all her close relatives had moved to Oaxaca City.

I had been warned by Villaltecos not to take sides in political and personal disputes. No one asked me to take sides, and I did not. But I was required to participate in village work committees within which the disputes were being enacted. I also spent many social evenings with the district court judge and civil recorder. Curiously, the judge had been stationed in Villa Alta when I was there in 1973, later left, and then returned in 1984 just one week after I did; both of us were back in Villa Alta for the first time in ten years. His open discussions of his views about law in Villa Alta and his responses to village politics and personal alliances informed my research. The civil recorder was a native Villalteco and one of the few residents of the seat who participated in the regional assemblies.

As I listened to the developing disputes I realized that their most common vocabulary was that of the morality tale and the dispute tale—stories told about the past and present behavior of opponents or allies and styled to influence the evaluation of opinions and arguments voiced in disputes. Such tales, often interpretations of events and relationships commonly known and discussed among Villaltecos, contained both myth and fantasy, yet they communicated the character of the players. The disputing process thus consisted of tale and counter-tale spun in group discussions and telegraphed around the village by way of the networks of kin, friends, and neighbors who formed the voz pública.

In this nonviolent participatory process, it is not surprising that Villaltecos evaluated disputing parties on the basis of their conformity to local codes for passing information and on whether they resorted to other means of disputing such as violence. I found that certain basic rules governed the passing of information. Direct responses to direct questions were given only to close associates; even family members were sometimes shut out. The person holding the information being sought controlled the whole conversation and its topics. Direct requests for information were to be expressed only once in the same conversation; the person sharing information voluntarily was not to be interrupted; and tales were not to be used outside the context of an ongoing dispute. Sharing tales was an invitation to alliance and, if the alliance was accepted, required a reciprocal response. It was all right to try to get others to misuse information by making misleading statements. However, misuse of information was a signal that the misuser had renounced an alliance or that the alliance did extend into all matters. Finally, the greater the power of an individual the greater the latitude he had to use information in ways that violated the rules. Deciding whether an individual could misuse information was a process of evaluating his or her power.

The themes of the morality tales included theft, overdrinking, promiscuity and infidelity, quickness to anger, use of violence, capriciousness, crime and corruption, and misuse of information. Whether a tale influenced the subject's status and power was determined not by the tale's accuracy but by how well it was conveyed and how well it was integrated into the subject's public identity.

A Villalteco who increased his political status by longevity or by overcontributing time or money to the village also enjoyed greater immunity from the effects of morality tales. Villaltecos could not obtain political status and power without first obtaining moral and legal privileges. Information created and shared by the politically powerful carried the greatest weight in the public voice.

It became clear to me that morality and dispute tales were used more often to prevent the accumulation of power, either in disputes or in village governance, than to lower the status of Villaltecos. Villaltecos could engage in behavior considered immoral without losing local rights or the ability to participate in the disputing process. The exception to this general rule was open opposition to participation in all forms of village maintenance or repeated neglect of civic duties.

Progressive leaders enjoyed greater moral privilege than did Calero leaders. For example, the murdered cacique Areli Fabela, a Progressive, had been known in Villa Alta for being *valiente* (brave) because he sometimes responded to disputes with other males by violence or threats of violence. Despite a general feeling against the use of violence, some in Villa Alta cited this characteristic as a factor that contributed to Fabela's ability to maintain authority.

How Villaltecos whose status was in question used information was more important than the information itself. For example, Villaltecos questioned the ability of the president, Otilio Espinosa, to assert authority and to carry out projects. He had switched his allegiance from the Caleros to the Progressives, and Villaltecos said he was capricious in addition to being quick to anger. But the primary focus of debate over Espinosa's competence was his use of the village public address system. His critics suggested that he misused it by providing too much information to villagers. Villaltecos use information to influence others. Espinosa, not a cacique, was attempting to assert too much authority.

One of the few Villaltecos who lost status as a result of moral violations was Amado Amaya, the son of Manuel Amaya, the former cacique. Both male and female Progressives and Caleros referred to Amaya as a lépero because he spread negative morality and dispute tales about his fellow Villaltecos without reference to local codes that regulated the development and sharing of information. He questioned the morality of others outside of the context of disputing. He told his tales anywhere to just about anyone, and he also shouted obscenities in public. He committed most of his offenses while drinking. Until his rehabilitation in the 1984 disputes, Amaya held no responsibilities in local governance and had no apparent influence in the development of disputes.

The disputes that took place in Villa Alta from January through June 1984 became interlinked as they developed. The initial forum for the first major dispute, between the padre and the seminarista, was the Ayuntamiento, the district seat's titular governing body. The president of Villa Alta often mediated disputes, and it was to the president that the padre went immediately after arguing with the seminarian about the church keys.

That the padre attempted to share his authority over the seminarian with President Espinosa was ironic on two counts. First, by village custom, employee disputes were resolved administratively, and the dispute with the seminarian fell in the administrative jurisdiction of the Catholic church.[1] Second, Espinosa could not play an impartial role because the seminarian was a friend of his family and the padre was his outspoken political opponent.

The president, far from helping the padre, allied himself with the seminarian, unilaterally adjudicated his innocence, and turned the dispute into one between the padre and the municipio, claiming that the padre had made false charges. Other friends of the seminarian also came to his defense and treated the dispute as one between the padre and Villa Alta, suggesting that the padre had misused his position both in Villa Alta and in its neighboring villages.

Only then did the padre take the route of village custom and manage the dispute by moving the seminarian out of his church position. But by calling in the president the padre had already transformed the dispute into one between the church and the municipio.

The women's network, supporters of the padre, treated the dispute as one between the village and the seminarian, questioning whether he had abused his church position and misled Villaltecos. Thus the women placed the dispute in the realm of the voz pública. The women, the padre, and members of the seat government then entered into negotiation in the public voice over the roles of the padre and the seminarian. This negotiation also involved the delineation of the relationship between the church and the village.

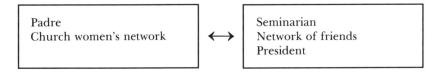

Padre		Seminarian
Church women's network	⟷	Network of friends
		President

The dispute spread to the state when the padre went to the ministerio público with accusations of theft against the seminarian.[2] He could have placed the accusations before the municipio and allowed village authorities to decide whether to appeal the case to the district court. That course, however, would have put him back up against President Espinosa.

The state, through the ministerio público, responded as both a political and a legal institution. The ministerio público, who could exercise wide discretion in his decision, took testimony but claimed to find insufficient evidence to prosecute the seminarian.[3] The padre's supporters characterized this decision as a stall motivated by politics and tried to put pressure on both the ministerio público and the district judge. The judge, by his statement, *"No me consta,"* showed that he was in agreement with the ministerio público. The prosecutor's actions, in turn, fueled President Espinosa's accusation that the padre had raised false charges, and the judge's opinion gave weight to moral accusations against the padre based on his misuse of information.

The Catholic church's banishment of the seminarian from Villa Alta did not remove him from the dispute. Villagers continued to negotiate his identity.

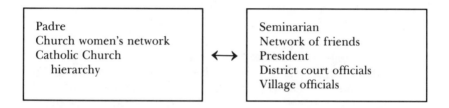

The municipio increased the church's role in the dispute with the escrito, signed by municipal officials (the síndico and others) and sent word to the bishop in Oaxaca City, requesting removal of the padre from Villa Alta. While Espinosa denied signing the escrito, he had once again attempted to arbitrate the dispute, this time reaching a decision on the relationship of the padre to the village. The padre's supporters responded by changing Espinosa's role from an authority figure to an opposing party in their dispute. Many villagers felt that the president had reached a decision prematurely, and they questioned his ability to use authority.

The matter of the padre's identity and his relationship to the village now assumed greater prominence in the disputing process. Villagers linked the dispute between the padre and Espinosa to an even larger dispute: the one between Caleros and Progressives over the finances and activities of the fiesta of the Santo Intierro. This linkage brought village urbanites into the dispute and changed its nature from one between individuals and their respective dispute-activated networks to one between groups within the extended village. It also changed the nature of the information processes. Villagers began to evaluate the padre, Espinosa, and the Caleros and Progressives in terms of alternative futures.

This process of evaluation led to the creation and telling of moral tales about numerous Villaltecos as part of the process of creating clear indicators of symbolic identity by which villagers could evaluate or rank the various stands within the now interconnected disputes. Through a common language of disputing, Villaltecos personalized the various organizational components involved in the dispute and made them accessible to the extended village for ranking. To contain and resolve the disputes Villaltecos had to decide which dispute tales to give precedence. In this way they guaranteed that the outcome of the disputing would be a group-based choice that would affect the future direction of the village. The opposing stands of the Caleros and the Progressives introduced cross-group associations and the challenge of ranking them as well through the disputing process. Thus villagers began to organize disputes and dispute tales on the basis of the quite accessible relationship between Caleros and Progressives.

The impact of Calero stands became clear during the fiesta. The Caleros who controlled fiesta planning increased the padre's authority in village affairs and acquiesced in his ban on the Friday night dance. For a while the Caleros seemed to be on the defensive. The performance of many fiesta events remained in doubt as a result of lowered quotas, and Progressives argued that they could have done a better job of organizing the fiesta. But as the fiesta got under way Progressive leaders faded into nonparticipation; their opposition was expressed primarily through Espinosa, who vetoed municipio cooperation with the fiesta committees.

The show of power by Caleros during the fiesta, when the guest band serenaded the Caleros but bypassed the Progressives, increased tensions within Progressive families. As Progressive men argued against the padre, their wives and daughters supported him. Family kitchens were scenes of discussion and argument over the roles of the padre and Espinosa in the village.

The padre, at the same time, was using the church, a focal point of the fiesta, as a forum for making political points by bringing in his friends in the clergy to talk against the separation of church and state. And Espinosa was attempting to show power by arresting Villaltecos for public drunkenness—a tactic that backfired after the fiesta when the women of the village linked the arrests to the president's dispute with the padre.

The power of urban networks was demonstrated as village urbanites became active leaders and participants in fiesta events, to which they contributed as if they were village residents. Calero urbanites lobbied strongly in favor of the padre as the padre's allies from within the church argued for greater participation of the Catholic church in local political affairs.

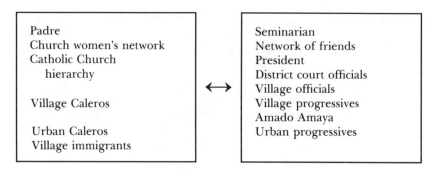

Another event also linked the local disputes to the city and introduced a new player. Amado Amaya's article in the Oaxaca periodical criticizing the padre was seen as a violation of disputing procedures, a misuse of information, and a movement of the dispute out of private village channels into a public forum. As a consequence, Villaltecos did not initially enter the information into the public voice. Nevertheless, the article did prompt Villaltecos to explore Amaya's accusations against the padre. Although Amaya had been relegated to deviant status as a consistent misuser of information, he was at the same time a latifundista and the son of a former cacique. His action against the padre, though criticized by many Caleros and Progressives, also elicited some Progressive compliments on Amaya's courage.

A man of contradictions, Amaya had made a clear statement and moved himself to the center of the disputes. Through the success of his crops, Amaya represented native Villalteco access to the resources of the external world. His entrance into the political fray forced consideration of his role in the context of Villalteco power relations. Thus the Villalteco who stood as an example of moral deviance entered the disputes as a major opponent of the representative of external moral authority and respectability.

In his article Amaya charged the padre with violating the boundaries between church and village by seeking local political power. He also presented the padre as a violator of the traditional clerical role by asserting that the padre had had sexual relations with young women. Thus, as the padre was moving to the center of Villalteco politics and intergroup disputes, Amaya and the villagers who believed his tale were creating a means for making the padre marginal.

After the fiesta, information about the disputes continued to develop. In the village junta the women supporters of the padre expressed their opposition to Espinosa. Espinosa then challenged the women to make public the information they had been circulating privately about the padre's charges of theft against the seminarian.

Because that would have meant going into the district court as witnesses, the women declined to take a public stand. They had little faith in the legitimacy of the court, which they saw as a political tool.[4]

The arrival in Villa Alta of district villagers representing the regional assemblies to protest the jailing of a fellow villager was important to the ongoing internal disputes of the seat. The protest reminded Villaltecos that new political alignments were forming in the district and that those involved in the alignments were attempting to influence the district seat's political and legal role. These outlying villagers were actively competing to influence district court decisions by new political means.[5] Formerly, only Villaltecos had been able consistently to assert influence in district agencies.

At this point the disputes had reached a high degree of complexity. They seemed to be taking place on at least three levels, with each tier representing a different type of conflict within the dialectics of the village and the external world.

The first tier involved conflicts between the Caleros and the Progressives. I call it the tier of externalities. The second tier had its foundation in the opposition between the men and the women of Villa Alta. I call it the tier of custom. The third tier, the tier of identity, arose from familial and personal differences between various individuals and groups—the cross-group social matrix through which disputes developed.

In the tier of externalities Caleros and Progressives disputed over the roles of village residents and the external world in village affairs.[6] The Caleros favored diminished authority for "landed" Villalteco families and greater political participation by the Catholic church, nonnative district seat residents, and neighboring villagers. They wanted a village that was closed to state political influence yet more open to the political concerns and movements of the region. Although Caleros were inconsistent in their stands on the local development of state-funded projects, they generally opposed projects that required villager contributions and voluntary labor. They were also inconsistent on what role Villa Alta should play in the district, but some of them thought its role should be diminished.

In contrast, the Progressives opposed participation of the external world in village affairs except through state-funded projects and state district offices. They supported mediation of state-village relations by local brokers who achieved their positions of authority by contributing time and financial resources to the village. They argued for mandatory participation in the cargo system and other forms of voluntary service required under traditional village civil law. Outsiders and nonnative residents, they argued, should gain authority in the village only by climbing the cargo ladder.[7] They wanted to confine church authority to the church grounds and to increase Villa Alta's political leadership in the district. In principle, though often not in practice, both the Progressives and the Caleros opposed the use of state force in Sierra village political conflicts and disputes.

In the tier of custom, men and women were in opposition as a result of male ties to the external world and female control of the traditional codes and processes by which local status was defined and achieved. The women had fewer opportunities than men did to obtain personal power through the political, economic, and bureaucratic systems of the external world. But the women generally controlled the creation, development, and sharing of information.[8] The women spread the personal dispute tales and moral histories and remembered and gossiped about villagers' descent—potent political information, since Spanish descent was important in obtaining political power in Villa Alta.[9] In this information process the women sought to exclude information that came from the external world and in this way opposed both the Caleros and the Progressives.

In opposing external influence over local disputes the women exerted a conservative force in the village legal system. At the same time, by using local codes to preserve status distinctions of birth, wealth, and occupation, they were a force of legal evolution. They facilitated an open legal system in which all villagers familiar with local information processes could participate.

Before 1974, the women of Villa Alta maintained strong social relationships among themselves that helped defuse conflicts among the male political groups and between generations. This source of feminine influence diminished with increased migration of native Villaltecos to urban centers and a resulting increase in exogamous marriages. In 1980, when women assumed the role that male mayordomos had played in the Catholic church, they found both a new reason and a new place for socializing that overrode political conflicts among the men in their families. Thus the church had both social and political value for the women.

Women achieved power by influencing moral status. The system of status gradations which they guarded was, along with the cargo system and caciquismo, a source of local power and influence. The women's information helped determine who could move to the higher cargo rungs, including village president, and who could achieve permanent political power that superseded both cargo and moral obligations. Politically powerful men depended on the women to circulate favorable stories about them, to deny unfavorable stories, and to withhold information that could be politically harmful.

All Villaltecos participated in the tier of identity. In this tier disputes were personal and tended to escalate or to remain unresolved. They had many sources: conflicts within and between families; historical conflicts over land; status-based antagonisms and resentments resulting from economic, occupational, and descent-based social differences; and sexual rivalries and violations. Some of these disputes stemmed from conflicts between former and present caciques and their supporters. These conflicts had widened with the weakening of the consanguineal ties that joined the families of political rivals and with the growing perception of a threatening external world. Thus disputes in this tier gave both social organization and historical depth to the political and philosophical differences that characterized the conflicts between Caleros and Progressives.

As I watched the disputes of 1984 grow in complexity, I realized that the conflicts that fueled them varied over time. Sometimes the disputes escalated within the tier of externalities as both Caleros and Progressives used the padre, the seminarian, and the president to symbolize their political differences. At other times, they escalated within the tier of custom as the women ostracized the seminarian, supported the padre, and lobbied the district court officials. At all times the historical conflicts in the tier of identity added a personal tone and heightened the emotions of the disputants.

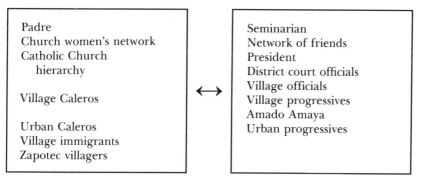

A resolution of the interlinked personal, religious, and political disputes finally came when Villaltecos attached them to the secular dispute over Amado Amaya's appointment to teach at the ETA. Although the ETA was located in Villa Alta, its students and faculty had become increasingly linked to the other district villages.[10] It represented the growing power of these villages, which Villaltecos considered antagonistic to the district seat.

As the ETA conflict grew Villaltecos simplified the disputes by defining them through just two composite symbols: the padre and Amaya, both of whom had been accused of violating the village's information code. By choosing the local symbol of external morality to represent threats to the village from the external world and the local symbol of immorality to represent internal order and village boundaries, Villaltecos were able to invert the relative positions of Amaya and the padre and eliminate barriers to resolving the disputes.

The padre, who disliked Villaltecos and preferred the outlying villagers, came to symbolize to Villaltecos the power of the other district villages and the possibility that some Villaltecos would ally themselves with the leaders of these villages. The padre also was at the center of the conflicts between men and women, both Calero and Progressive. With the development of the ETA dispute, in which some Villalteco students at the ETA openly opposed their fathers, the padre also came to represent a challenge to the authority not only of village governance but also of the family.

Amaya, on the other hand, represented native Villalteco families in opposition both to other district villages and to church involvement in village politics. He represented the secular world of agricultural expertise and professionalism as an avenue of achievement for Villaltecos and a source of their distinctive identity and power in the district. Amaya's major supporter, Mario Fabela, represented Villa Alta's role in the establishment of the ETA and the seat's former power in school-related issues. Fabela's support was significant, since the public voice insisted that Fabela's brother had been killed by opponents in other district villages as a result of his role in founding the ETA. Villaltecos remembered that this involvement of other villages in Villalteco politics had resulted in violation of village boundaries by the state and had sparked the internal division of the village and the rise of the Caleros to power (Parnell 1978b).

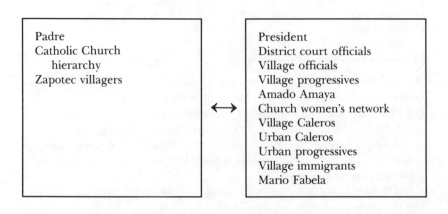

Padre	President
Catholic Church	District court officials
hierarchy	Village officials
Zapotec villagers	Village progressives
	Amado Amaya
←→	Church women's network
	Village Caleros
	Urban Caleros
	Urban progressives
	Village immigrants
	Mario Fabela

Women of the village now entered the information from Amaya's articles into the public voice. They confirmed that the padre had engaged in relations with young women in Ocotlán and said that the Catholic church had discriminated against Villa Alta by sending its worst padre to their impoverished district as punishment. Thus the public voice, with the padre's previous supporters among its most active participants, moved the padre to the margins of the village and transformed his role as moral authority into one to be evaluated within local processes of moral judgment. Villaltecos then decided independently of the state and the church that the padre should leave Villa Alta.

In moving the padre to the margins of the village, Villaltecos also moved the internal contradictions he generated and the external forces he represented to the realm of the disorderly external world, giving them a lower priority in the local scale of values than internal forces, which represented the traditional village principle. And by moving Amaya into a bureaucratic position, villagers resolved the organizational and processual contradictions he represented. They placed him in a realm of social order where other Villaltecos with such secular training also resided. He then fell under the jurisdiction of the village's ETA parents' association, an organization that represented the connection between the traditional Villalteco family and the bureaucratic organizations of the state and nation.

Villaltecos ultimately agreed to define the 1984 disputes within the tier of custom. Conflicts between men and women and between the internal and external worlds provided the only ordered system of codes, symbols, and processes accessible to most villagers. These conflicts were managed by individuals who were relatively impartial in the political conflicts of the village.

Had Villaltecos ultimately defined the escalated disputes as political issues they would have relegated them to the realm of disorder that characterized the tiers of externalities and identity. The disputes could then have developed in at least three ways. First, Caleros and Progressives could have continued to use their external alliances to strengthen their authority. This pattern was followed by the groups in neighboring villages that formed regional and Protestant assemblies (see chapter 5). Second, the disputes could have led to a greater exercise of authority in village affairs by the church (if the Caleros had gained the upper hand) or the state (if the Progressives had gained the upper hand). This outcome would have provided only a temporary imbalance in village negotiations, for the power of the dominant group would have derived in part from external groups whose power interrelationships were in flux. It also would have diminished the importance of village democratic, legal, and political processes. Third, the disputing could have continued through the same or new vehicles for articulating interpersonal and political conflicts.

In contrast to the political conflicts between Caleros and Progressives and between generations of politically powerful males, the conflicts between men and women offered villagers a clear choice between the external world of disorder and authority and the internal world of clearly ordered statuses and clearly articulated processes for achieving and evaluating them. The district seat actually was a microcosm of the external world in its occupational, political, and cultural pluralism, and thus the local system of law and morality could be used to bring order to both local conflicts and conflicts generated by Villalteco ties to the disorderly system of external authority. Conflicts among males both expressed and were fueled by external disorder, while conflicts between males and females offered a choice between the disorder of village male ties and the relative order of female society and the familiar systems of status and morality.

The women of Villa Alta were forced to make a choice between the padre and Amaya. If they had continued to support the padre, they would have been allied as well with those who threatened Villalteco control over the ETA, Villa Alta's political role within the region, and local systems of achieving authority. The women thus struck the ultimate bargain that managed the ongoing disputes. In exchange for dropping their support of the padre, local codes and processes that women represented achieved priority in ordering dispute relations.

Women maintained their power in Villa Alta, though urban migration continued to threaten it. Their influence lay in a moral legitimacy that was grounded in social ties. These ties were facilitated by the church and cut across the political divisions that were identified with externalities. As keepers of the codes and the knowledge that regulated the achievement of local authority, women provided the church as a social system with a local political role it could not achieve under the leadership of external authority.

Both male and female Villaltecos placed the symbols of the external world and the conflicts over their relationships to these symbols in a secondary role to their support for Amaya. Caleros and Progressives, including Espinosa, joined to support Amaya as a successful reflection of their views on the village and the native Villalteco family—their first allegiance in the spreading disputes that involved forces of the external world.

Resident and urban Villaltecos
District court officials
Catholic Church hierarchy

Padre
Zapotec villagers

In sum, the resolution of the 1984 disputes was a move toward increased internal centralization for the district seat. Neither the church nor the state gained authority in the village. Villaltecos ordered relations among the officials and institutions of the village, state, church, and region by using only local legal processes to lower the status of the padre. Social roles and institutions that had become of ambiguous value as a result of external disorder and local political conflicts were placed within the clear-cut external-internal dichotomy represented by male-female conflicts.

In this way, the concept of the extended village and its control and representation by native families achieved top priority in the rankings formulated as a result of disputes and their resolution. Church and state were given lesser rankings as allegiance to Amaya took precedence over that to the padre and local legal codes took precedence over the state legal system. Other district villages were placed lowest in the ranking. Villaltecos viewed these villages as their greatest external threat. This perceived threat brought local political opponents together and lessened the perceived ideological distance between the two political groups that represented the historical Mexican conflict between church and state.

CHAPTER 5

Village Divisions and Regional Alliances

The view up the mountainside from the district seat was especially tempting. My room was on the front porch of a house that, in 1973–74, was occupied by a large Villalteco family as part of a larger extended family compound. From this room I was able to see the old village of Temazcalapa nestled in the crescent of a mountain ridge that soared upward from the river at the base of Villa Alta's mountainside. I could also see traces of the high village of Taguí, frequently obscured by clouds.

At the invitation of some residents of Taguí, I began to make three- and four-day visits to this Zapotec village of about 500 persons, four hours by foot from Villa Alta. Research there provided a relaxing diversion. I worked in the maize and coffee fields alongside the residents. They answered my questions while we hoed and weeded. It was not the most effective way to conduct interviews, but it was the only way to talk with the villagers alone.

Villagers of the Villa Alta district say that the ground has a spiritual quality and that by walking on the soil a person learns respect for the lives it has nurtured. I had heard the story of Jaime García, an electrician from Oaxaca City who, while working in Zoogocho, killed a villager. The villagers decided to try to teach him respect for life. They removed his shoes and walked him barefoot to the district court in Villa Alta. García did indeed learn his lesson, for, allowed freedom to work in the village while serving his sentence in the two-room dirt-floored jail, he brought electricity to the district seat. He also married a Villalteca and became a respected citizen.

In the 1970s many spiritual messages were being carried along the paths of Villa Alta—not only from the Catholic church, whose messengers had long walked these paths, but also from newly arrived Protestant groups. At that time Taguí was unique in the marketplace region because about half its residents had joined the Jehovah's Witnesses. Witnesses from Oaxaca City traveled ten hours by bus to Lachirioag, then walked to Taguí to give Bible instruction. In turn, the people of Taguí journeyed to Oaxaca City to receive instruction and monetary gifts sent from the Watchtower, the Witness headquarters in Brooklyn, New York.

Taguí was the first of the villages north of Villa Alta to experience a widespread change of religious affiliation. Although men were the titular leaders of the Witnesses, women were a significant influence behind the conversions of their husbands and sons. Some families were split, most often on the basis of female participation in Witness instruction and male participation in Catholic activities. Some men participated in both—to appease their wives, some said, while maintaining Catholic male social life. Behavior that had been the norm among females of Taguí was now becoming the norm among males, that is, no smoking and little drinking. More and more the Witnesses were becoming the anchor of village activities.

Male Catholics of Taguí discussed the benefits of converting. They noted that men who had participated in the Witness faith over the years had improved their financial situations by collectivizing agricultural activity and accumulating capital to spend on work animals. Their mules rather than their wives and children now carried firewood from the base of the mountain up to their houses in the village.

The Witnesses duplicated some functions of Taguí's primary school. Even Catholic men spoke favorably of teaching the children Spanish with the Witness Bible as the text. Many adult women also had achieved literacy in this way. In addition the Witnesses provided an alternative to the village and state authority structures for dispute settlement. Disputes among Witnesses were taken to the sect's local authorities. From there they could be appealed either to Witness authorities in Oaxaca City or to the village court and the state legal system. But this judicial alternative did not mean that the Witnesses completely rejected village governmental authority. They participated along with Catholics in the secular cargo system, fulfilling their obligations as village citizens through voluntary service. Cases that affected the village, such as a 1974 case of theft of village funds, were settled in juntas (which both Witnesses and Catholics attended), according to the village custom of restitution.

As Taguí became more and more non-Catholic the residents abandoned the collective autonomous political and Catholic village unit. They also diminished exchange relations with other district villages, including participation in traditional fiestas, and thus Taguí's regional ties of exchange weakened.[1] But the residents reformed as a collective Witness unit within their larger centralized religious system tied to the external world. They moved into an ethic that valued both individual mercantile and collective agricultural activity directed toward the development of capital or surplus.[2]

Between 1974 and 1984 eight Witness families from Taguí moved to Villa Alta. Members of four of these families opened dry-goods and vegetable stores and *fondas,* or small restaurants. Others took manual jobs with state institutions. Three of the immigrant entrepreneurs built new homes in the contemporary rather than the traditional style, using fired bricks imported from Oaxaca City.

By 1984, when I returned for my second period of study, most Catholics of Taguí had converted to the Witness faith. The conversions were accomplished with little conflict. The Witnesses did not set up replacements for the Catholic and fiesta ties they had broken with other district villages, but they did take over the reins of village government and maintained local autonomy. Though isolated from its neighbors, Taguí increased its ties to Oaxaca City and to the Witness organization at national and international levels.

The Protestant groups of other religiously divided villages of Villa Alta, whose conversions were more recent, experienced greater conflict with their Catholic neighbors. Unlike the Witnesses of Taguí, many claimed, on religious grounds, the right to withdraw completely from participation in the cargo system and other aspects of village governance. Financial contributions came in from Evangelical and Pentecostal organizations in the United States to their members in the subsistence villages of Yetzecovi, Yatzona, Yetzelalag, Temazcalapa, Reaguí, Yaée, Yalahui, and Yaa. Only four villages in the marketplace region of Villa Alta remained undivided by religious conflict—Betaza, Camotlán, Roayaga, and Lachirioag. Seat residents claimed that the presence of three Catholic nuns in Camotlán mitigated against conversion to Protestantism. Roayaga, like its ally Villa Alta, enforced the rule that villagers of all religions had to observe the same civil law. Groups in Lachirioag that sought political change were influenced by politically active teachers from INI (Instituto Nacional Indigenista).

In 1984, the influence of these Protestant conversions on the everyday life of the district seat was quite evident. Villaltecos and other villagers told me tales of enforced curfews, new laws against drinking, and precious objects stolen from the Catholic churches. The paths from these villages to Villa Alta were less traveled than they had been during my first stay because the villagers participated less often in Villa Alta's weekly marketplace. But they increased their communication with sources of authority outside the regional Catholic church and the state government offices in the district seat.

Conflicts between religious groups centered on the duty of fulfilling cargo obligations, the interpretation of village and state law, and the separation of church and state. While church and state conflicts were not new to these villages, the conflicts now assumed added significance as part of a larger political debate over the division of allegiances and resources among state, village, and church. Concern over such disputes grew as Protestant conversions increased and as international Protestant organizations assumed a larger economic role in the villages. Two legal cases that traveled to the district seat from outlying villages in the first half of 1984 illustrate the nature of the disputes.

In the first case, Protestants from the village of Yatzona charged in January that village authorities had unlawfully jailed and tortured them. The same month, after the charges were reported in a Oaxaca City newspaper, the village authorities, who had been visiting the capital, found themselves waiting in line for the bus to Villa Alta with the ministerio público (district prosecutor). With the exception of the plaintiffs, the major parties in the case were to travel together to Villa Alta.

Once the bus was well into the peaks and ravines of the Mixe district, the Yatzona authorities entered into an informal discussion of the case with the ministerio público. A Villalteco teacher along for the journey acted as a go-between. The teacher, a native of Villa Alta and a brother-in-law of the mero cacique, David Mendiolea, had been assigned to Yatzona before moving to Oaxaca City. The teacher heard the authorities deny that they had tortured the Protestants and starved them for the seven days they were in jail. The authorities said they were correct in jailing the Protestants as citizens who refused to comply with their village obligations.

The teacher knew that in Villa Alta persons who did not participate in work projects or comply with fiesta cuotas and committee assignments were not usually jailed but were given other options, including paying a fee, hiring someone to take their place, or paying a fine. He suggested that the village authorities did indeed have the right to seek compliance from citizens and that Protestants should fulfill village obligations, but that torture, denial of food, and jailing for seven days was wrong.[3] The síndico of Yatzona argued rather loudly that if the Protestants did not fulfill their obligations he had no obligation to extend village services to them. Nor could he provide them with protection from any actions other villagers might take.

After this discussion the síndico talked with the ministerio público, his counterpart on the state district level. Their conversation was much quieter. Afterward the ministerio público, who may exercise discretion in the processing of a case and may, through procedural delays, slow it down, decided to use these tactics in the case of the Yatzona authorities. He did not exercise his prerogative of jailing them to take testimony when they arrived in Villa Alta, and six months later none of them had been confined or formally apprehended.

In the second case, word reached Villa Alta in March that the Catholic church of the Mixe village of Tonaguia had been robbed. The culprit had not yet been identified, and Villaltecos joked that a Catholic could not have stolen the valuable gold objects because Catholics were not dishonest. The village conducted an investigation that resulted in the placing of accusations before the ministerio público against the village president, a Catholic. The president refused to leave office and resisted apprehension. Villaltecos then stated that the president must have viewed the theft as a political act.

Another case of theft proceeded quite differently. In June 1984, the Catholic church of Lachirioag was robbed. As in Tonaguia the people of Lachirioag conducted their own investigation, but they did not report the case to the district court. The investigation revealed that the thief was a teenage male, a native of Lachirioag. He was convicted in a meeting of villagers and sentenced to hang. He was buried in the Lachirioag cemetery.[4]

I made frequent visits to Lachirioag, a Zapotec village only fifteen minutes by foot from Villa Alta. The warmth and charm of its people beckoned me away from the complexities of field research in the district seat. Lachirioag was not without its conflicts, but unlike Taguí and several of the other marketplace villages, it acted them out in the political rather than the religious arena. The political battles between church and village that divided Villa Alta had spread to Lachirioag. Some of its leaders had established political alliances with Juan Calero. In Lachirioag, Calero and his allies urged a larger political role for the Catholic church and a diminished role for teachers from INI. The Lachirioag faction that fell under the influence of INI teachers was aligned with regional assemblies. It challenged the ruling national political party PRI, though without forming ties to other national parties. It also opposed Villa Alta as the seat of a Zapotec district.

The ideological and political schisms of Lachirioag mirrored those in other divided marketplace villages. The residents of Villa Alta's closest neighbor were the most articulate organizers for indigenous rights in the region. Along with the seat ally Roayaga, the peasants of Lachirioag shunned coffee as a cash crop, preferring corn and sugarcane. They had earned a reputation for being the region's best farmers. They were relatively free of patronage ties to Villalteco moneylenders and merchants and the past influence of Villalteco teachers.

Though they were ardent Catholics, many residents of Lachirioag called for the primacy of a political organization within the municipio libre that would be capable of actively opposing, through peaceful means, all nonregional, non-Zapotec influence. Thus these Catholics, living in a village where the traditional civil-religious hierarchy had deteriorated relatively little and where caciquismo had not taken hold, found themselves opposed to the Catholic politics of Calero and his local lieutenants. The allies of Calero held power in the cargo system and the Ayuntamiento at the beginning of 1983.

The November 1983 issue of *Topil,* the official publication of the regional assemblies, was published by the villagers of Lachirioag and devoted to the village's recent confrontation with state authorities. In space set aside for political comment a citizen of Lachirioag wrote:

> The capitalist system and our country's present crisis have given rise to the existence of extreme abuses, excesses and frauds, ambition and envy, confrontations and disturbances in disputes. Such is the situation of the village of Lachirioag, which from October 16 to November 16, 1983, has lived through an important period of intense struggle borne in an organized and united way in defense of the rights and customs of the internal life of the community. It was no longer possible to support the traitors of the village; they were removed, and in the course of the struggle certain objectives were reached: the unity, the organization, the active and direct participation, the solidarity and the organized response which the village gave to the police and bureaucrats who came to repress the citizenry of this village. In spite of them, the spirit of the struggle is not dead and will continue along its path until victory.
>
> For Lachirioag, 100 per cent pacifist for years prior to today, it is important not to become alienated from the present problem. Such problems exist also in various communities. Some struggle to free themselves from the impositions of the PRI government; others, as a result of the influence and domination of a minority, continue suffering internally.

October 16 was the day the village of Lachirioag dismissed its president and handed over his responsibilities and those of the elected authorities who served with him to a new group. Although the change of authority did not take place in accordance with rules governing village elections, it did accord with the consensus of the villagers.

Problems had been brewing for some time as citizens in opposition to the president grew in numbers and strength. They eventually listed the following complaints and demands:

1. Since taking office the president has entered no monies into the municipal treasury.
2. Without consulting the village the president has attempted to change the village's system of education, replacing Zapotec-speaking teachers employed by the Instituto Nacional Indigenista with the "formal" system of education of the state.
3. Without reason the president and some of his supporters assaulted the authorities of San Juan Tabaa.
4. Since January 1983 the authorities have been absent from the village for periods of one week to fifteen days without the consent of the village, their last exit being November 5, and their whereabouts are still unknown.
5. They have not informed us about the truck which the federation gave to Lachirioag and neighboring villages.
6. They made some elected members of the Ayuntamiento sign false documents. They also placed an announcement in the Oaxaca newspaper *Noticias* in which they lied, saying that within the municipal building there was an amount of 260,000 pesos plus a 150,000-peso contribution that the village had made and set aside for repairing the church. They also said that villagers had burned the archives of the Ayuntamiento. All of this is completely false.

Following this, villagers protested energetically against the three authorities who are the cause of our problems, and the opinion of the villagers is as follows:

a. We do not wish to change from the system of indigenous education, since while our school has been in their hands we have noticed changes.
b. We should be given a report on money received for the truck.
c. We should be given a report on fines received.
d. If the [former] authorities do not render such reports, their property within the community should be seized.[5]

Beyond the above particulars, perhaps the primary complaint against the elected authorities was that they had aligned with the

Caleros and had consistently followed Juan Calero's counsel. Calero and a few of his strongest supporters were teachers in the state system, which many villagers opposed. Some Caleros leaned toward the political strengthening of other district villages, but they also argued for greater allocation of village funds to the church. Although Lachirioag was a Catholic village most of its citizens were not prepared to give more power to the church by allocating all village funds to it. Calero was aligned with a Oaxaca faction of PRI, his close ally being the son of the former mero cacique Raul Torres, who served as an assistant (*subgobernador*) under the former governor of Oaxaca. Calero was also well known in Villa Alta for using state law enforcement resources to impose his own policies.

On the night of October 27, two platoons of state police arrived without prior notice at the municipal building of Lachirioag. Their mission, as the people of Lachirioag stated, was to apprehend or kill the newly installed president and his supporters and to take over the Ayuntamiento. When the police arrived one of the village authorities ran to the church and rang the bells to assemble the villagers. They gathered quickly at the municipal building and confronted the police, contending that the new president was backed by the village. The police stated that according to the Mexican Constitution the actions of the villagers represented subversion. The villagers and the police stayed the night in the municipal building. The next day the police left Lachirioag after the people suggested that the proper authority to respond to the village's problems was the state Department of Governance, not the state police.[6]

On November 1, two lawyers from the Department of Governance arrived in Lachirioag. But the villagers with whom they met determined that they were allies of the dismissed authorities and had come to oppose the newly appointed president. The lawyers asked the new authorities to sign papers, but they refused. The lawyers then left Lachirioag.

The next day the village named a five-man commission of citizens and teachers to travel to Oaxaca City and Mexico City to meet with citizens from Lachirioag who lived there. They also were to lodge a complaint (*demanda*) against three members of the dismissed authority in the offices of the state attorney general and the prosecutor for state governance.

In Mexico City, the commission handed copies of their complaint to the office of the *procurador general de la república* (attorney general). Then on November 6, the commission convened a meeting of Lachirioag citizens in Chapultepec Park. About one hundred and fifty persons attended and discussed the events that had transpired in their

village. The commission played tapes that had been recorded in Lachirioag meetings to show that a local consensus on dismissing the
village authorities had been reached.

After agreeing with the changes, the urbanites picked representatives from various parts of the city and appointed a *mesa directiva,* or
commission, to represent the Mexico City voice of Lachirioag. Following the meeting the commission returned to Oaxaca City for discussions with Lachirioag urbanites there.

A citizen of Lachirioag later wrote of the events in his village:

> We all know how the representatives of the government arrived
> in our village, wanting to trample us underfoot, but thanks to the
> courage of everyone, we confronted them, because for a long
> time they have come taking advantage of the ignorance of our
> forefathers, making us do things that we didn't have to do. But
> now we will never accept those impositions, now that we will
> continue to act in accordance with the voice of the village.

Thus the villagers of Lachirioag responded to the crisis in their
relations with the church, the region, and the state by asserting traditional village values. They rejected an authority that placed alignments
with the state (the PRI and the Caleros as they were viewed in Lachirioag) and the Catholic church above the village principle that sanc-
tioned decisions based on participatory democracy and authority
gained through voluntarism. Local conflicts started the organization of
urban migrants as villagers spread information about the conflict to
urbanites. The villagers of Lachirioag applied information and the ties
it activated to respond to representatives of the external world who
were backed by coercive force. Through *Topil* they spread information
to strengthen alliances newly formed in conflicts with the church and
the state. In using information to negotiate and extend the conflict into
the external world while asserting the principle of the village, villagers
of Lachirioag extended village-based law, its concepts and processes,
into the spheres of the region, the state, and the nation.

While changes in religious affiliations signaled the advent of issues
through which village conflict and a clear movement toward open
village boundaries were expressed, changes in dominance of political
parties did not represent a new direction in village affairs. The new
affiliations to political parties that offered alternatives to PRI in district
villages represented no change in relations with external institutions.[7]

To give villages and village parties and factions political labels like
PRI or PSUM (United Mexican Socialist Party), even though they may

maintain alignments with national parties, actually obscures their stands and leanings. The political division in Villa Alta illustrates the difficulties. There, both sides received support from, and in turn supported, PRI officials. PRI is much like the Catholic church in the district—it experiences local variations though under the same leadership and policies. These local political variations would exist in the villages even without the PRI label, for many are expressions through village society of conflicts among urban and state institutions that are in contact with village life. Others express a dialectic between urban and peasant life.[8]

The foundation of politics in the villages is the village and its maintenance. Village opposition groups—those that prefer stronger village boundaries and rejection of the agencies and programs of the state and nation as well as those that favor loosening boundaries to facilitate the entrance of externally generated projects—can appeal to PRI in their efforts to control the direction of village choices. It is unlikely that a political party could, through noncoercive policies alone, strongly influence village choices.

The historically divided villages of Betaza and Yalálag (which are outside the Villa Alta marketplace region) serve as the most common examples of the dynamics of village dualism in the district. Between 1974 and 1984 one opposition group in each village chose to symbolize its interests by establishing alliances with a political party (PSUM) that opposed their local PRI-aligned opponents. But Villaltecos told me that the divisions in both Yalálag and Betaza were continued expressions of historical disagreements within village bands and were instigated by Catholic priests.

The division of Yalálag (de la Fuente 1949) is famous in the district, for it has been less controlled than Betaza's. It has been marked by greater political expression and has more often developed into violent confrontations. In 1974, the division of Yalálag into disputing barrios competing for power resulted in homicides that were reported to the state district court in Villa Alta. In 1984 Yalaltecos were expressing their division through new symbols. Yalálag is the only village in the district with two presidents, the result of the resolution of a conflict in which both sides claimed an election victory. One Yalalteco group was building on the division to challenge PRI and to align with the newly formed regional assemblies.

In Betaza, in contrast, local political bosses have controlled the political division since the early 1930s. Local lore describes Betaza's division as a violent one. Betazanos maintain close ties to the district seat through native families who moved to Villa Alta and through

Betaza residents who own land in the seat. Villaltecos claim that ties to the seat strengthened the rule of Betaza's bosses. The past two generations of Betaza's political bosses have come from the Cartucho family, the father joined in the last decade by his son Jacobo. Only seven families in Villa Alta hold large tracts of land. These large landholders are, with one exception, the caciques and the sons of former caciques. Of these landholders, the Cartuchos of Betaza hold the largest tracts. The elder Cartucho and his sons also own retail stores in Oaxaca City. Like the political boss of Villa Alta, David Mendiolea, they rule their village from Oaxaca City through local deputies. The Cartuchos are aligned with PRI and with Mendiolea.

In the same election in which PRI control of Yalálag was weakened, Cartucho rule of Betaza was challenged with the election of a non-PRI president. In Betaza, the division apparently produced violence. The new president disappeared and a Cartucho supporter was installed in his place. Villagers of both Betaza and Villa Alta suggest that the challenger was killed and that Cartucho had a hand in it. In 1984, because of fear of retaliation, Cartucho was unable to return to his village and his mobility even within Villa Alta was severely limited even though the ministerio público had not filed charges against him.

The struggle in Betaza is not over freedom from the dominance of centralized parties or governance. Both the Cartuchos and their opponents support village autonomy and oppose external participation in village elections. The Cartucho opposition also participates in regional assemblies, which support village independence and oppose changes in village collective organization as a result of outside intervention.

The regional assemblies of the Sierra were formed at the end of the 1970s as a response by village authorities and factions to growing challenges to the traditional village concept based on the cargo system, juntas, and cuotas. Assembly representatives meet periodically in a participating village to discuss problems of individual villages, to exchange information that might help resolve these problems, and to reach administrative decisions. Oaxaca City networks are important fields of information exchange for assembly participants. The assemblies respond as a support organization to events and problems that arise in participating villages and factions, they publish *Topil,* and they maintain a fund to respond to political and legal problems.

The regional assemblies can be termed a confederacy of villages. They are most similar to regional marketplaces, with the currency of exchange being information rather than vegetables and dry goods. As centralized bodies that organize village surplus (funds) and formulate regional and indigenous political and legal policy, assemblies provide an alternative to the dendritic market structure in which administrative and marketplace centers overlap. Assembly policies challenge the legitimacy of Villa Alta as an administrative center. Assembly participants come from throughout the district and from Chinantec and Mixe villages of neighboring districts. Ideologically and pragmatically, the assemblies are responses to the growing divisions in the villages. Their policies are aimed at the institutions and groups considered to be sources and instigators of village divisions—primarily political and Protestant institutions. The primary goals of the assemblies are to maintain and increase the autonomy of the Sierra villages by refurbishing village-based customs. They seek to strengthen village boundaries against the involvement of outsiders in choice-making on the village level. Thus they would preserve and strengthen village authority.

Villages and factions are relatively equal within the nonhierarchical assembly structure. Villages divided along political and religious lines do not participate as villages within the assemblies but are represented by factions and identity groups. District villages which are not divided, such as Camotlán and San Francisco Cajonos, are the major organizational forces, regional meeting places, and nodes of communication in the assemblies. In these villages, service in municipal offices and assembly participation overlap.

The assemblies are primarily an indigenous and Catholic network of villages and factions which, through reference to local tradition, cooperate to strengthen local rule against external political, religious, and economic institutions. Indigenous identity, rather than being Zapotec, and reference to shared customs appear to be the major points of commonality among assembly participants. The assemblies in the district of Villa Alta cross-cut districts and language-based identities through the participation of both Mixe and Chinantec villagers from the districts of Choapan and Zacatepec.

Assembly participants recognize shared problems which they identify as threats to the political autonomy of the village. However, the assemblies do not group these threats together as part of a larger system which is inherently evil. They are not opposed to a specific type of political or economic system but rather resist any external incursions on local rule and custom.

Some villagers trace assembly networks to the more politicized and ideological coastal Zapotec city of Juchitan. They trace Juchiteco networks to other Central American countries. If new components of political ideology are forming in the Oaxacan networks that have traditionally overlapped in the marketplaces of Oaxaca City, they are not expressed in the regional assemblies of Villa Alta. The political foundation of the regional assembly is the corporate village, and its goal is local control over external institutions.

The report of the regional assemblies in November 1983 listed the following objectives:

1. To reestablish community unity, which those who consider us inferior have tried to destroy.
2. To resist the imposition of customs foreign to our reality by those who do not understand our village organization.
3. To resist foreign penetration.
4 To resist the imposition of outside authority and religion that is not in accordance with village processes of choosing authorities on the basis of community service.
5. To preserve our culture.
6. To resist being the subject of medical experimentation by North Americans.
7. To resist discrimination.
8. To improve means of communication (roads and telegraph service).
9. To resist division of villages by outside force.
10. To advance, little by little, in defense of our culture.

Among the forces recognized by the assemblies as major external sources of village problems are the national political parties that attempt to influence local elections, the Catholic church and Protestant groups, and the United States as the home base of religious organizations, an ally of national political parties, and the source of medical experimentation.

Assemblies are a new level of integration of Sierra political groupings. But the magnitude of change represented by this new level of village organization is not as great as may appear at first glance. An old friend of mine from the Sierra, a teacher born and reared in a Zapotec village who had moved with his family to Oaxaca City, visited me one day in Villa Alta. He saw my copies of *Topil* and began to read them. When I asked him what he thought of them he replied, "They're all gossip." Indeed, the regional assemblies are an elaboration on village information-sharing mechanisms, such as the voz pública, that are used to manage internal problems. Their major tool is knowledge, and their ideology is that of the cargo system.

Regional assemblies developed during the same decade that many villagers of Villa Alta's marketplace region converted to Protestantism and that several villages developed political divisions. Many of the village groups that joined the assemblies were opponents of either

Protestant groups who refused to comply with local civil law or political groups closely aligned with PRI and local political bosses.

The village concept provides the basic system for organizing social relations. Through village values the forces of religion, politics, and law are interpreted and interrelated. These values delimit the ways in which the outside world can participate in the village. The parameters, or pragmatic norms, within which the church and the state can function in the village are established through consensus on village jurisdictions and villager rights.[9] Jurisdictions and rights, in turn, are established through customary expectations on the roles of insiders and outsiders.

The village concept also influences the ways a village enters into the outside world. The Sierra village is an extended village, with its urbanites representing a state and national organization that is developing alongside traditional political, legal, economic, and religious institutions of the centralized state and nation. Federal and state organizations have provided the contemporary paths along which the village has ventured into the world beyond its geographic boundaries. But the village itself has influenced the content and impact of these paths.

These two forms of state and national development—the extension of centralized systems into the village and the extension of the village into centralized systems—provide both villagers and state officials with clear alternatives as they choose their lines of development. They are parallel paths, interconnecting the same fields of opportunity and problems, yet traveled in opposite directions. Along these paths are crossover points where travelers may change directions and alliances, moving either toward the application of the village concept and principle to state and national institutions and processes or toward the application of the state concept and principle to the village with greater participation of outsiders in village affairs. The first direction—internal centralization—leads to maintenance (or, in some villages, reconstruction) of the village concept and village autonomy, the development of new local associations that interpret the policies of external institutions, and the elaboration of village law and legal processes. It is the path that we have seen the district seat taking (chapters 2 through 4). The second direction—external centralization—leads to decreased local autonomy and the weakening of village boundaries, but also to the development of legitimate regional administrative organizations. Most of the villages in the Villa Alta marketplace region are taking this path.

Because the district seat's historical and contemporary pluralization makes it in many ways a microcosm of the external world, Villaltecos are able to draw on a broad range of information and symbols in meeting the challenges from outside. Their marketplace neighbors have fewer ties to urban and state institutions and more homogeneous local and extended populations. As they engage in the process of negotiating external and internal order out of perceived disorder, they are faced with a narrower range of information and symbols, even though they, too, are able to draw on the ties of the extended village. To develop information about their village's relations with the external world, the Zapotec villagers expand beyond their local and extended village associations and create new ones. Those who seek closer association with outside institutions and lessened ties to village civil processes enter into Protestant assemblies. Those who seek stronger village boundaries and greater local control join regional assemblies.

The most characteristic function of the regional assemblies is the sharing of information. Through the cooperative development of information they reach a common identification of the negative components of the external world that seem to threaten their villages. The assemblies also develop strategies for managing threats. They are nonhierarchical organizations of equal political units that are attempting to replace at the regional level the weakened leaders of divided villages as negotiators on behalf of the village with the external world.

CHAPTER 6

State Law or Village Law

In 1973–74 the focus of my research was on the relations of Zapotec villagers with the Oaxaca state legal system and with the district seat of Villa Alta, where the state district court and other state offices are located. I spent about six months at a desk in the court in Villa Alta gathering case materials from the voluminous archives. Cases in the archives reach back to the 1600s, and the idea of dedicating my entire research to documenting and analyzing cases across that broad expanse of time was tempting. Court officials urged me to do so. But, while much remains to be added to the already extensive record of Mexico's past, the study of contemporary Mexican village life and of relations between village society and the regional and state systems has been neglected. Extensive longitudinal studies of aspects of the village life of minority indigenous populations have been conducted in some areas, but the role of the region and the state in the life of the peasant village today remains a little explored field of research. That is why I decided to focus on current disputes in the Zapotec villages of the Sierra de Juárez as well as in the Spanish-speaking district seat.[1]

Toward the end of my first year I traveled to all the villages in Villa Alta's marketplace region. I conducted interviews with village presidents, secretaries, and caciques. By this time my presence in the district was well known, and villagers did not appear disconcerted even when I walked into their village in the middle of the night, having avoided a steep ascent in the heat of the day. Although the Villaltecos

warned me to stay out of most of these villages and certainly not to
venture into them alone, the villagers were quite willing to answer my
questions about their village life, legal processes, and appeal of cases to
state courts. The most valuable information I gained from them was
straightforward explanations of their avoidance relations with Villaltecos and the state legal agencies in Villa Alta. All disliked the Villaltecos because the district seat residents considered themselves superior to other villagers. In spite of similarities, each village seemed like a
social island extending from its location in the Sierras to Oaxaca City
but bypassing the other villages and the district seat.

These interviews were important when I coupled them with the
cases I read and the observations I recorded in the district court and
the interviews I conducted with marketplace villagers in the district
seat. The most obvious aspect of relations between the district villages
and the district court was that most villagers did not cooperate in the
processing of appealed cases, and they developed strategies that often
thwarted the court's investigations. These strategies centered on the
control of information provided to the court or the withdrawal of
cooperation in the provision of information.[2] In stark contrast to their
behavior in village courts and juntas, villagers in the district courtroom
were passive and reticent. In every case in which the accused had been
apprehended, attempts by the district judge to initiate discussions
between the accused and the complainant failed. Such discussions are
meant to be the very foundation of court negotiation and mediation.
Most cases were left hanging without disposition and now rested on the
floor of the archives.[3] Since I was starting from scratch, however, these
cases were a good primer on state legal processes and their relation to
village dispute settlement.

Village judicial officials, as we have already learned, hold voluntary
positions in the village legal system. The same is true of the state system
of appeals. The village síndico is a subordinate of the district ministerio
público, who is a salaried employee of the state and a subordinate of
the state procurador general. The village alcalde is a subordinate of the
district judge (in the Juzgado Mixto de Primera Instancia, the state
district court of first appeals), and the judge is a subordinate of the
president of the Tribunal Superior del Estado de Oaxaca in Oaxaca
City. A village president may choose to act as administrator of the
village legal system and mediate disputes either along with or instead
of the alcalde. We have seen that to be the case in Villa Alta, where the
president generally mediates interpersonal disputes.

Villagers and village officials may appeal disputes to the district
court. Villagers may also initiate cases in the district court rather than
in village courts. District court officials conduct their own investiga-

Table 1
Villa Alta Marketplace Villages

Village	Population 1973	Distance Hours by Foot	Cases Appealed[4] 1963–73
Lachirioag	2556	0.5	16
Betaza	1994	2.5	13
Temazcalapa	1678	2.0	4
Yaa	1025	1.5	23
Yatée	748	2.0	5
Camotlán	737	8.0	3
Yatzona	597	4.0	1
Reaguí	505	9.0	1
Roayaga	497	2.0	5
Yalahui	359	3.0	2
Taguí	339	4.0	2
Yetzelalag	286	9.0	4
Yetzecovi	225	2.0	1

tions into cases (*procesos*) in Spanish, taking original testimony from the accused, the plaintiff, and the witnesses. (The appendix outlines the structures and processes of the Oaxaca state judicial system that apply to the appeal of village disputes.)

Between 1963 and 1973 neither village size nor proximity to Villa Alta had a noticeable effect on the frequency of appeals of local disputes from the thirteen villages in Villa Alta's marketplace region to the district court (Table 1). All villages used the district court infrequently. Based on a search of court archives, the total number of disputes appealed annually from all forty-nine settlements that appealed cases to the district court was about fifty, including cases the court did not prosecute. Factors that did appear to increase the frequency of appeals were village schisms and weakened local leadership.

Table 2 relates village structure to the tendency to appeal cases and the ability of villagers to control the flow of information about disputes from the village to the district court. *Stratified convergent villages* have a relatively low potential for cohesion because of a history of competitive and hostile relationships among the native villages of migrants and cultural differences among migrants. These factors weaken information control.

Synthesized convergent villages have experienced an influx of migrants in search of land and refuge from political problems. There is occupational homogeneity, and villagers have not organized themselves into

Table 2
Villa Alta District Villages—Organization and Tendency to Appeal*

Structure (Example)	Leadership[5]	Tendency to Appeal[6]
Stratified convergent (Villa Alta)	Nonaligned political bosses	Yes
Synthesized convergent (Camotlán)	Aligned political bosses	No
Historical convergent (Talea)	Representative elected officials	No
Divergent (Juquila Vijanos)	Representative elected officials	No
Homeostatic (Tabaa)	Political bosses (and elected officials)	Slight
Homeostatic (Temazcalapa)	Elected officials	No
Divided (Yalálag)	Nonaligned political bosses	Yes

*From Parnell (1982)

groups based on place of birth. Control over information flow is strong.

Historical convergent villages were developed by migrants and continue to accept outsiders. Their population bases, however, have endured over generations. They are not factionalized on the basis of population groupings. Ties among individuals crosscut groups. Control over information flow is very strong.

Divergent villages have spawned smaller settlements. Residents have split away from these villages because of overpopulation, political differences, or a scarcity of land close to the village nucleus. The exodus of residents to form new settlements that in practice are autonomous lessens the potential for dissension in these villages. Control over information flow is strong.

The residents of *homeostatic villages* are united by crosscutting ties that tend to control dissension and lessen threats to village cohesiveness. Powerful political bosses appoint allies to positions in village governments. There is little movement into these villages. Control over information flow is strong.

Divided villages contain political factions led by political bosses. In Yalálag, the political groups are also endogamous neighborhoods. The villages have nonrepresentative governments. Control over information flow is, at times of overt conflict, weak.

In the ten years between my two stays in Villa Alta, village social control weakened as schisms between village-based groups widened and villages divided along political and religious lines. Although the foundations for these schisms were already present in the villages' relations with the external world, over this period (1974–84) the effects developed into a marked challenge to local cohesiveness. Village groups and factions strengthened their ties to external religious and political organizations as they assumed the identities of these organizations at the local level. In seven villages of the Villa Alta marketplace region that divided on the basis of religion, Protestant groups mounted direct challenges to local secular authority by refusing to comply with local civil law. All these villages were within six hours by foot from Villa Alta.

Nevertheless, district court officials stationed in Villa Alta, including the civil recorder, told me that the frequency of appealed cases had not increased since 1973; Villa Alta continued to be a peaceful district that demanded only a small amount of legal casework. The district judge stationed in Villa Alta in 1984, who had also served there in 1974, noticed no change in his caseload. Even during the first six months of 1984, a period of intense confrontations between village officials and Protestant groups, villages appealed only two religious disputes.

Thus during my second stay in Villa Alta one question stood out: Why did the villages of Villa Alta choose not to explore and create alternative social order through the formal disputing processes and centralized bureaucratic agencies of the Oaxaca state legal and political systems? The answer to this question lies in how the villagers use their disputes—the functions of disputing in village society.[7]

Legal anthropologists have developed several concepts and frameworks useful in describing and understanding the choices individuals and groups make among legal alternatives. Most anthropologists who have studied the role of law and social control in society use the dispute as a unit of analysis (Llewellyn and Hoebel 1941; Colson 1953; Gulliver 1969, 1979; Collier 1973; Nader and Todd 1978). Lawyers and sociologists who have broadened their studies of law beyond the processes of official or formal legal systems and have searched for links between informal social control and the use and development of formal law have also enjoyed the dispute as a unit of social analysis (Abel 1973).[8]

Analysts most often define the dispute as a conflict gone public. Gulliver (1979, pp.75–76) distinguished between a dispute and a disagreement. Whereas disagreements "are commonly resolved within a relationship (sometimes by terminating it) by dyadic and private problem-solving between the parties themselves," a disagreement becomes a dispute when a person "attempts to take the disagreement out of the private, dyadic context and to put it into a public domain with the intent that something must be done."9 Therefore, when a disagreement or a conflict becomes a dispute,

> there is some kind of public recognition and cognizance of the matter and of the desire for attention. Some other people become involved as supporters, advocates, or representatives of each of the parties and perhaps as third parties. There is a publicized proposal that the matter be dealt with through some recognized, overt procedure that is routinized in some degree.

One factor influencing disputant choices is the fit between the principles expressed in dispute settlement processes and the principles that guide other forms of group-based interaction. The legitimacy of law and a legal system in the eyes of a group depends on two factors: the content of the law and its relationship to group norms, and the processes realized in the application of the law and their relationship to the social principles applied in group-based interaction. Legal processes, like norms and ideals, express the principles that govern relationships and should be expressed in the content of legitimate law.10

Relationships between social principles and processes are important in the analysis of legal systems. How people in groups evaluate these systems influences the choices they make as they evaluate and manage their disputes. For example, the Ndendeuli of Tanzania, as described by Gulliver (1971), are accustomed to negotiating their disputes. To do so they draw on social alliances and information about political, economic, and social relations. They would find the process of adjudication, with its strict rules that narrow the evidence related to a dispute (Nader 1969a, Fuller 1971), in contradiction to the principles that govern their daily relationships and a hindrance to their continuation.

Groups may match or associate different processes of dispute management with different problems and kinds of status relationships. For example, group members may define and manage disputes that arise in the group quite differently from disputes between group members and strangers. They may manage disputes between leaders and followers differently from those among followers.

As members of a society match processes with problems they rank these processes according to their value for the society. One kind of dispute settlement process may achieve legitimacy or respect and usefulness within a society because it realizes principles that underlie social relationships. In the relationship between disputants and the larger society, this process will be integrative or cleansing. On the other hand, members of a group may direct problems or individuals considered most threatening to the social order into processes that do not express valued social principles and that taint or pollute those who go through them by their illegitimate nature (Garfinkel 1956).[11]

There are then two distinct types of dispute settlement processes. One kind does not change the social statuses of disputants because it does not remove them from ongoing social relationships. By expressing the principles that underlie such relationships, this kind of process is integral to these relationships and therefore to the society. A second kind of dispute settlement process does change the societal status of disputants. It applies principles that are not integrated into ongoing social relationships and thus are external to the fabric of valued ties to others.

As a society becomes more complex, variation across what are seen as legitimate processes may increase. Disputants may employ a wide range of principles in the dispute settlement process in a search for definitions of their developing relationships. The settlement process itself may play an important role. As the relationship between parties changes during their enactment of a dispute, their dispute may move from one process to another. For example, an urban couple in the United States may seek mediation through a marriage counselor to resolve problems if they decide they want to continue the relationship. Should their problems continue after counseling they may seek to sever the relationship through a court process of adjudication. The relationship between the parties as a disputing dyad may become more important to dispute development and to the legitimacy of processes than the relationship between disputants and larger social and political groups.

How disputants become involved in a settlement process may influence their relationship as well as their group-based statuses. If members of a group choose to take their dispute to processes and authorities considered illegitimate by their group, its negative evaluation may taint or pollute them. No matter what the disposition of their dispute within the process, group members may consider the disputants guilty of normative violations. On the other hand, if legal authorities who have not gained their power through legitimate means impose a settlement process on group members, then neither involvement in the process nor involvement in the disposition may influence the statuses of disputants in the eyes and words of their peers.

Thus several factors influence how a legal process may affect a dispute relationship. Foremost among them is the match between the principles that guide the dispute settlement process and those that govern the relationship. How the dispute relationship is conceptualized, that is, how the disputants and their respective groups define and view their relationship, also has an influence. Another important factor is how disputants enter into settlement processes. This factor is directly related to authority and the process of attaining it.

The principles that permeate group-based social relations also govern the process of communication. They establish, as components of law, who has a right to information, who can use it in what ways, and how individuals in various statuses or social positions can acquire it.

The process of disputing is a process of developing information with which disputants and their reference groups will define their relationships. Through the disputing process information is developed, acquired, and then applied to the definition of the statuses of the disputants. Group culture includes norms that govern the processes of sharing, using, and developing information. Informational norms govern social processes, such as gossiping (Gluckman 1963, Todd 1978) and problem solving. The information one may share—and with whom and about whom—is a factor in the definition of rights and duties across social roles and groups that form the fabric of social life.

Analysts have characterized dispute settlement processes in relation to information. For example, the evidence considered relevant to a dispute varies from one process to another, as does the strictness of rules governing evidence. The Kpelle moot in Africa (Gibbs 1963) and the village court of Talea in the Villa Alta district (Nader 1969a) are classic examples of processes that admit both a wide range of participants as sources of information and a wide range of information about disputant relationships. Rules governing both the range of relevant information and who may introduce information into the processes are loose. For the Kpelle and the Taleanos, factors related to the past, present, and future of disputant relationships are integral to understanding the nature of a specific disagreement that has entered into public forums.[12]

Rules governing the kinds of information that can enter formally into a formal process of adjudication and who can provide the information are stricter (Gulliver 1979). They focus less on the past and future relationship between the disputants and more on their behavior in the specific dispute as it is defined in written law. Analysts of judicial processes in the United States have pointed to the fact that although strict rules of procedure govern bureaucratized legal forums, cultural stereotypes and the demands of bureaucracy enter into the case-related processes of assessment and evaluation that influence the judgments of third parties (for example, Farrell and Swigert 1978, Mileski 1971).

A wide range of evidence and information may then enter into processes with both loose and strict rules of evidence. Differences lie in who may enter the information and how it is integrated into the settlement process. In a loose process like the Kpelle moot or the village court in Talea, the development and use of information in the field of law is a public right available to all who conform to the recognized social principles regulating group membership. In a strict process like an official U.S. or Mexican courtroom, the provision and evaluation of information is a privilege gained by conforming to principles associated with the special roles of information development, transfer, and use in centralized formal legal systems. In the village court, information is legitimized as a public good; in the courtroom of official law it is a private good.

The field of law may provide disputants with many settlement alternatives, both official and unofficial. How and whether these alternatives are organized into a legal system depends in part on how disputants use information—whether the information gained in one is or can be applied in others, whether this information is applied overtly or covertly, and whether each process generates its own information according to the distinctive principles of the social and legal structure in which it operates.

How the processes of legal structures develop and apply information relates directly to whether these structures become integrative systems of law, achieving legitimacy both across and within groups, or whether they become systems of law that grow only through intergroup and intragroup divisions. How legal structures develop information in and for the use of settlement processes relates directly to whether and to the extent to which they must use physical force along with information to achieve conformity to the laws they espouse. Information and physical force are interchangeable in the field of law; but, just as in the simultaneous ingestion of aspirin and alcohol, the effects of both are altered when applied together to the problems of a social system.

Should an authority or third party enter into an information-sharing process without occupying a position that gives the right to enter (in disputant or group perspectives), the relationships among those participating in the process will be immediately changed by the violation. Their relationships may change in many ways, but there will certainly be a response to the violation or a dispute over informational rights as a result of the illegitimate sharing or acquisition of information. The principles governing the flow of information will be in dispute.

Therefore, in relation to information, the way disputants enter into a settlement process and who enters into the process will be evaluated by parties and their respective groups in the context of norms mapping the flow of information across statuses and settings. The informational evaluations of disputing, like evaluations of the match between principles that apply to relationships and processes, will influence the legitimacy, acceptance, and application of outcomes reached in settlement processes.

When disputants can choose from among more than one legal system, their perceptions of the legal order—how the authorities and the information developed within the systems interrelate—influence how they define their disputing relationship and how they choose to manage it. Group-based perceptions of legal order influence group patterns of dispute settlement. Thus the actual and perceived relationships among legal systems or alternative processes of dispute settlement relate to the development of legal processes and systems. In evaluating their choices, disputants compare the principles they apply to group interrelationships with the principles that appear to interrelate legal processes and systems. In this way they match the legal order and the social order through the choices they make as they manage their problems.

A perception common to early anthropology was that small groups of people, such as tribes and peasant villages, who are culturally homogeneous in comparison with complex Western societies experience little stratification or pluralism and little separation or perceptual distinctions within their systems of law, politics, economics, kinship, and religion. Kinship ties, for example, were seen as the definers and carriers of all other forms of cultural information and material exchange—the unifiers of social and cultural systems, all of which were blurred together in the popular consciousness through the idioms of kinship and religion.

Many decades of additional research have revealed that members of tribes and villages do indeed distinguish—in perception, choice, and social ties—among systems of relationships, such as those that are economic and those that are religious, and they apply different normative evaluations to each system (Moore 1973). Pospisil (1967, 1971), in a comparison of law in several societies, found that individuals in tribes and villages may develop customary modes of distinguishing among forms of social relationships and may extend these distinctions into the field of law. Each subgroup in a society, such as the family, may develop its own legal system.

Pospisil's definition of a legal system extends its study beyond the boundaries of the bureaucratic state. According to Pospisil (1967, p. 9), "the totality of the principles incorporated in the legal decisions of an authority of a society's subgroup constitute that subgroup's legal system." Pospisil then argued that "every functioning subgroup of a society has its own legal system which is necessarily different in some respects from those of the other subgroups." From the differences among norms that govern relationships within different types of groups arise differences in law. As group authorities state these norms with consistency over time in reference to the same types of relationships, the norms become law, expressing and supporting the principles underlying group-based ties.

Pospisil developed the concept of legal level to delineate a dynamic of law that exists in all groups. Recognizing that the legal systems of a society vary according to their "inclusiveness," some claiming or holding jurisdiction over a larger number and broader variety of groups than others, he argued:

> Since the legal systems form a hierarchy reflecting the degrees of inclusiveness of the corresponding subgroups, the total of the legal systems of subgroups of the same type and inclusiveness . . . I propose to call legal level. As there are inevitable differences between the laws of different legal levels, and because an individual, whether a member of an advanced or a primitive society, is simultaneously a member of several subgroups of different inclusiveness, he is subject to all the different legal systems of the subgroups of which he is a member.

Pospisil's recognition that a member of any group participates in different legal systems helps clarify an important dynamic in the development of legal systems recognized by Collier (1973) in her study of Zinacanteco law in Chiapas, Mexico. She found that legal systems develop in response to the choices of individuals among the many legal systems in which they live as they attempt to manage their disputes. Dispute settlement choices influence the nature of legal systems, the types of cases these systems handle, the relationships they define, the laws they develop, and their relative force in the relationships of a society. The underpinnings of legal development are those forces that influence or canalize the choices of individuals as they attempt to manage disputes.

Disputant evaluation of a settlement process relates to its frame of reference, which may be either the relationship between and the goals of disputants or the relationship between disputants and the larger society. Several studies of dispute settlement consider the match between process and disputant relationships and goals (Colson 1953; Nader 1965, 1969; Ruffini 1978; Collier 1973; Nader and Todd 1978; Mather and Yngvesson 1980–81; Gulliver 1971, 1979; Aubert 1963; Gluckman 1967; Felstiner 1974). Nader (1969a) showed, for example, that in Talea the maintenance of ongoing relationships and their protection against the harm of escalating disputes are goals of dispute

settlement. The villagers maintain important relationships of cooperation and reciprocity. The costs of severing such relationships are great,
so the litigious Taleans frequently employ compromise, a process that
may repair relationships threatened by disputes. Village authorities at
times force those who are unwilling to accept the principles of compromise into village-based adjudication or the district court in Villa Alta.

In the district seat of Villa Alta and its marketplace region, villagers
perceived and experienced changes and disorder in intergroup relations in the 1970s and early 1980s. They perceived relations among
social groups in the village, the region, and the larger social universe as
threatened or threatening. This larger context of social order and
disorder influenced how disputants defined their relationships and the
purposes to which they applied their disputes.

Interpersonal disputes expanded into intergroup disputes.
Through disputing villagers both tested and created social and legal
order. The disputants generally chose and elaborated processes that
generated the broadest range of social participation and information
about groups. In the processes of mediation and negotiation villagers
could create and evaluate information about groups through common
codes without experiencing formal sanctions. Because they were ordering relations among social and legal institutions that varied widely
in material power and organizational principles, villagers most often
chose processes that expressed the social principle of the village. This
principle grounded participation in village affairs in contributions to
village development. It granted villagers the authority to assert order
within a social universe that seemed out of control.

In defining their relationships, disputants may refer to different
social contexts since, as Pospisil (1967) argued, they may at one and the
same time be participants in more than one legal system. All the legal
systems in which disputants participate may be inherent in disputes in
any one system. Disputants evaluate the dispute relationship not solely
in terms of the subgroup in which it is developing but also in terms of
other subgroups in which they can participate.

The context of reference may influence the type of information
disputants seek about the dispute. If family members in a dispute
define their context of reference as the bureaucracy, they may expand
the dispute to the bureaucracy or to third parties who represent bureaucratic interests in search of information about the relationship
between kin and bureaucratic ties. Mather and Yngvesson (1980–81,
pp. 778–79) in their discussion of dispute transformations characterized the process of dispute expansion in this way:

Expansion refers to a rephrasing in terms of a framework not previously accepted by a third party. Expansion challenges established categories for classifying events and relationships by linking subjects or issues that are typically separated, thus stretching or changing accepted frameworks for organizing reality. . . . We argue here that the expansion of individual disputes is one way that social change is linked to legal change.

Disputes can expand as disputants or third parties introduce new substantive concerns or reinterpret related disputes from the past. Disputes may also expand through a form of escalation. As disputes escalate they expand through the incorporation of individuals and groups who symbolize or represent new issues and subjects and possible linkages among them. Escalation provides a social component for dispute expansion, and the context of actual relationships through which disputants can act out, explore, evaluate, and manage new linkages among individuals, identities, and groups. Escalating disputes provide contexts of comparison of the past and possible new disputant relationships.

There are risks inherent to the escalation of disputes beyond the immediate social and political contexts of disputant relationships. Though escalating disputes may provide arenas for legal innovation (new linkages among subjects and issues), they may also introduce into disputes power relationships that extend beyond those between the initial disputants or those among disputants and a third party in a moot or courtlike setting. In the mentalistic or logical exploration of new social linkages in the setting of a court or moot, the process of evaluation and ratification may be a response to the prior formation of these linkages in society, or may precede a process of testing new relationships in future cases.

As disputes escalate through and across social systems, new alliances or linkages may form so that disputants can evaluate them. Dispute escalation may initiate the process of evaluation. Control over dispute escalation lies not only in the ability of disputants to form new social relationships and alliances but also to withdraw from or sever them. In this way, escalating disputes, as processes of exploration and experimentation, may spawn disputes as participants continue to search for suitable relationships and sever those they have rejected.

Three basic contextual conditions may influence both whether a dispute escalates beyond the type of empirically discoverable relationship (kinship, bureaucracy, community) in which it develops and what new relationships it may grow to include. The first is the presence and accessibility of dispute settlement processes and third parties in the original context. That is a social, structural factor related to whether or not the original disputing context produces third parties acceptable to both disputants. The second condition is the degree of integration among the legal systems in which disputants participate. If these legal systems are integrated by common principles and purposes, members of one may have both vested interests in and knowledge and information applicable to disputes that occur in others. If they are poorly integrated, information obtainable through the processes of one system may not inform disputes that occur in another and disputes are less likely to escalate across them as a result of disputant choices. The third condition is the perceived relationship among the legal systems in which disputants participate. If interrelationships among subgroups are ambiguous, disputes may escalate in the process of seeking information about them. Disputants may ask how resolutions in one subgroup will affect disputant relationships within or to others. If the ties across subgroups are ambiguous, disputants may also expand their disputes in search of more favorable outcomes than they can achieve in one subgroup or context, even though these outcomes may be in doubt. In this sense, dispute escalation is part of the process of disputant exploration for information about law and legal systems, a search for the differences and similarities across processes of legal levels.

Given the human propensity to create order where it is perceived to be absent (Glacken 1967, Douglas 1970, Adams 1975), the ambiguity of ties across subgroups may motivate disputants to escalate their disputes in the process of seeking and generating information that will clarify the ambiguity. Disputants can apply information gained through dispute expansion and escalation to the ordering and evaluating of legal systems. And, of course, disputes over these relationships among subgroups may develop as products of perceived disorder or ambiguity.

As disputants choose to move their disputes from one legal system to another, they make statements about preferences for third parties and the contexts in which different kinds of dispute relationships should be evaluated. Over time, these choices become patterns. Disputants order relationships among legal systems as they choose sources of information about them. If disputants in the situation of disorder are seeking information about relationships among groups, they are most likely to choose dispute settlement processes that produce the most information about groups and their interrelationships.

We may compare legal systems in relation to two types of inclusiveness—one based on power and one based on principles. Legal systems that have power independent of other subgroups may claim authority over them and use independent power to assert authority. On the other hand, members of subgroups may use the principles asserted by authorities in one to organize relationships within and among others.

The latter legal system, which provides the most inclusive principles and is used by disputants to order and rank relationships among the subgroups in which they participate or which they consider inherent in their disputes, is a centralizing legal system. It provides the principles that order relationships among groups in which disputants participate or could participate. As disputes escalate disputants make choices among various principles applied by authorities in the systems through which disputes pass. These principles applied by disputants in the management of the widest variety of disputes are, as a result of disputant choices, at the top of the hierarchy, or ranked highest, among legal principles. They provide the cognitive links through which disputants associate (order) and rank (evaluate) subgroups.

In this way, disputes provide a link between social organization and social order. The distinction drawn by Adams (1975) between levels of articulation and levels of integration is useful in examining this link in Villa Alta. Drawing on the work of Steward (1955), Starr (1954), and Wolf (1967), Adams (p. 158) contrasted a level of integration with a level of articulation:

> I (have) argued for a distinction between levels of articulation and levels of integration, using the first term to refer to the levels that may empirically be found in the courts of interaction in a society and the second to refer to the classification of levels that a society was likely to utilize in describing its own organization.

Levels of integration, Adams said, are the "empirically discovered levels of power differential within any part of the system under study" (p. 164). They exist in observable and measurable distinctions among the organizational units in a given society. They may be distinctive on the basis of interaction or content of interaction or on the basis of material differences and organizational structure.

Empirically discoverable levels of articulation in Villa Alta include:

family
village divisions
the village
the region
the district
the state
the nation

All these levels are represented by subgroups within the concept of the extended village.[13] The family and the village are the only social sys-

tems providing both the principles and the means villagers need to
mediate between the oppositions they encounter in the other levels,
oppositions to which local divisions are tied.

On the basis of material power, the Oaxaca state legal system is
clearly the most inclusive system of law in the social field of Villa Alta,
for it claims authority over the smaller subgroups and may draw on its
material resources to assert authority within them. In relation to organizational principles, however, the village is the most inclusive legal
system among the levels of law that form the social universe of the
extended village and regional assemblies.

Village disputants apply the principle of the village to order and
evaluate relationships among subgroups and the state. They use the
legal processes and the social principle of the village (replicated in
regional assemblies) rather than those of the state to generate information about the nature and relative value of village, regional, state, and
national subgroups. They apply this information to organize subgroups hierarchically as contexts of reference (and authority).

Adams (p. 80) elaborated on the level of integration:

> Both the people living in societies and the observers of societies
> find it necessary to classify sets of levels of articulation into larger
> classes, and the resulting system of conceptualized levels is what
> we are calling levels of integration. Levels of articulation are
> constructed out of the observation or recording of interactions
> and transactions among human beings; levels of integration are
> constructed out of data on levels of articulation, with some con-
> ceptual and cognitive dimensions that are brought to that data
> from our existing generalized cognitive map of the world.

Villaltecos, members of regional assemblies, and villagers of the
district in general choose the village rather than the state as the source
of principles for creating an integrated system of legal levels. The
village provides them with the processes of negotiation and mediation
through which they may test and participate in the creation of order
among groups that do not clearly value one subgroup or legal system
over others.

As we have seen, the Sierra village is a participatory democracy in
which authority is achieved through service in the cargo system, village
and Catholic church committees, village meetings, and village work
groups. In principle, villagers achieve authority by contributing time
and service to the village. Village civil law requires all adult males to
contribute. Village legal forums are similarly open and tied to such
information-generating processes as gossip, mediation, and negotiation. Through village dispute-settlement processes, villagers may ex-

pand their disputes in structured forums (in the absence of coercive force) and escalate them to explore possible evaluations of disputant relationships to other village subgroups and the larger groups of the world beyond the conceptual boundaries of the village. In doing so, they also explore the choices presented to them through contemporary symbolizations of the dialectic of the village—choices between the perceived nature of the external world and the village.

In creating regional assemblies, villagers have multiplied the village's resources for obtaining and evaluating information about the external world and defining the village's relationship to it. Both Villaltecos and members of regional assemblies from the outlying villages thus have chosen, within the village-external world dialectic, social authority over material power.

Cultural conflict characterizes the relationship between village and state law. Village legal principles, codes, and processes are not integrated into state law. Spanish rather than Zapotec is the language of the state court. In adjudicating disputes, state court officials assume authority over disputants—authority which villagers generally do not recognize as legitimate. Villagers generally do not apply state court decisions in defining either the local statuses of disputants (for example, as criminal or guiltless) or their interrelationships.

District seat residents of Spanish descent (in reference to language and chosen identity) experience less cultural conflict with the state than do their Zapotec neighbors. Like their neighbors, however, Villaltecos opt for village legal control. The state district court played no significant role in the management of the 1984 disputes in the district seat. Villagers integrated the state court into their local dispute settlement processes but did not allocate to its officials authority equal to or greater than that of local leaders.

Cultural conflict and the failure of state codes to integrate local codes into centralized legal processes are certainly important factors in state-village relations in the field of law. But the existence of these dynamics does not fully answer the question of why both Villaltecos and Zapotec villagers do not appeal more cases to the state.

The explanation lies in the relationship between the village and the larger world, which villagers perceive as out of control and threatening village life. Villagers define their local disputes in this context and escalate them in the process of generating social order. They choose to recognize most often the principles of the groups that provide them with dispute settlement processes through which they can create and participate in evaluating information about relationships among the groups and legal levels of the village and the world beyond its boundaries.

The Oaxaca state legal system, which relies on adjudication, does not provide villagers with processes through which they can expand and escalate disputes in the search for information about intergroup relations and innovate responses to changing conditions. The system rephrases disputes by what Mather and Yngvesson (1980–81, p. 778) call narrowing—"the process through which established categories for classifying events and relationships are imposed on an event or series of events, defining the subject matter of a dispute in ways which make it amenable to conventional management procedures." Officials in the Oaxaca legal system attempt to narrow disputes as they define and evaluate them in relation to state penal and civil codes. In adjudicating disputes, they are not concerned with the relationship between social ties and social order. Nor are they concerned with local perspectives on disputes and the broader past and future contexts of dispute relationships. They limit the relationships among issues, individuals, and groups involved. Court officials seek information they can relate to written categories and processes designed to determine the guilt or innocence of the accused party in relation to a specified act (Fuller 1971).[14]

The genius of village law lies in its elasticity. Working within it the villagers of Villa Alta are able to escalate peacefully their disputes and therefore order and dispute relationships among a wide range of social identities, groups, and institutions. The creative legal abilities of villagers shine most clearly in their use of daily disputes and local relationships to develop social orders that extend beyond the geographic boundaries of the village and into its larger social universe.

The factors that influence the choices villagers make among their legal alternatives are of course many. Their perception that the forces of social disorder lie outside the village is an important factor. But undoubtedly the most important is the widespread allegiance of villagers to the village principle of participatory democracy.

CHAPTER 7

Disputing and Centralization

The villagers of Villa Alta escalate disputes to generate social order in the same way one uses a flashlight to search for a key in an attic filled with life's mementos. These disputes are part of a larger social and cognitive process of exploration into the worlds of the city, state, and nation. Villagers make this journey along the well-traveled route of participatory village law. In the controlled and peaceful social forum of the negotiated dispute, they argue their various views of the world. Through escalating disputes they put together extended villages as piecemeal democracies that unite migrant and sedentary villagers in the creation of social order.

Village law is an adversary system in which leaders argue their views of the world to the villagers who speak in judgment. The disputants are not just postal official, schoolteacher, peasant, cook, aunt, or merchant. They are representatives of ways to arrange the world and enter the future. Villalteco disputants are tradition and change united by kinship and marriage and divided by the conflict of generations. The past and the future come together through what villagers bring to their disputes.

Some villagers locate the sources of their hardships outside the village and are motivated to explain and control them. Their tool in the process is society. They activate and expand the social ties of the village in search of information and symbols. They draw on social oppositions and new political alignments to debate and organize the roles of social and political groups. In the absence of oracles and libraries, they mine each other's knowledge of local philosophies, principles, and lives to evaluate various combinations of the old village and contemporary society.

Other villagers also locate the sources of their hardships outside the village but look within themselves for order. They enter into the hierarchical structures of Protestant churches and assemblies that preach self-control and, usually, withdrawal from village traditions and civil law. Rather than strengthening village boundaries as the regional assemblies attempt to do, the new Protestants strengthen their personal boundaries to elements of the external world. At the same time they build houses and initiate ceremonies in their own villages, then welcome Protestants from other villages as visitors. Like regional assemblies the new Protestant groups generate regional ties across villages, many of which formerly maintained inimical relations.

The responses of villagers to their perceptions and experiences of a disorderly and threatening world may be diagrammed in the following way:

Perception of disorder in intergroup relations	leads to	search for information about groups	leads to
development of information along lines of internal social differences	leads to	widening of internal social schisms	leads to
development of alternative cognitive orderings of social groups	leads to	evaluation of alternative orderings through disputing processes.	

When the primary disputing process is negotiation, as in these villages of Villa Alta, a second diagram is possible:

Disputing	leads to	the escalation of disputes to gather both political strength and information for negotiations	leads to
the formation of interest groups to evaluate and defend alternative social orders	leads to	coordination of competing groups through the processes of negotiation and centralization.	

In relation to the processes of negotiation and centralization,

Local stratification (differences among groups to be ordered)	leads to	local organization and symbolization of alternative social orders	leads to

localized
(internal village)
centralization.

   In contrast,

Local homogeneity (absence of marked cultural and economic differences among opponents)	leads to	regional organization and symbolization of alternative social orders	leads to

external
centralization.

The culturally plural and economically stratified district seat central-izes internally while many of its more homogeneous neighbors central-ize externally by taking their disputes into the wider world through the extended village, regional assemblies, and Protestant sects.[1] Villagers, however, have not increased their participation in the centralized sys-tem of Oaxaca state law, as we saw in chapter six.

   Nader and Todd (1978, p.13), drawing on the work of Colson (1953), Gluckman (1955), Nader (1965), Todd (1978), and Yngvesson (1978), diagrammed the relationships between the strength of social ties and the use of dispute settlement processes in this way:

Disputants in multiplex or continuing relationships	will rely on	negotiation or mediation in settlement attempts	which will lead to

compromise
outcomes.

Disputants in simplex relationships	will rely on	adjudication or arbitration in settlement attempts	which will lead to

win-or-lose
decisions.

It would not be accurate to say of Villa Alta that as village divisions and conflict over identity and value grow the villagers' ties change from multiplex to simplex.[2] For example, some political opponents in Villa Alta are close kin and work together in village projects and committees. In Taguí, husbands and wives and fathers and sons often participated in different religious groups, and Protestants and Catholics continued to work together in village governance. We can assume, however, that as villages divide and ties to external organizations in conflict increase, local ties weaken over time, even though they do not move from extreme strength to extreme weakness.

The relationship between disorder and village social schisms and conflicts influences the purposes of disputing. It overlays the disputes that escalate in spite of local control with a larger purpose than the resolution of interpersonal conflicts. These disputes become part of the conflict among village associations over alternative social orders for both the village and the external world.

In disputing over social order, systems of authority that are a part of the social systems perceived to be in disorder or out of control are in dispute, and so are interpersonal relationships. Disputants search for resolutions and order in alternatives to the processes in which disputed principles are imposed. In this case, the condition of weaker social ties does not necessarily lead to adjudication by established authorities. It leads rather to the use of processes that increase the authority of disputants in their arguments for new social orders and relationships. Negotiation serves this purpose, for it is a process in which the disputants themselves can continue their relationships as neighbors or kin in the absence of acceptable third parties (Gulliver 1979). Dispute escalation involves the search for information and alliances through which disputants can buttress their arguments in relation to those of their opponents.

The influence of social order on the disputing process in the Sierra village may be diagrammed as follows:

The disputing context of perceived external social disorder	leads to	magnification of differences within social identities of disputants	leads to
weakening of extant orders that define disputant identities	leads to	weakening of third parties of challenged social orders	influences

| disputants with either simplex or multiplex ties | to rely on | disputing processes that increase their social authority (to create social order) | leads to |

the use of negotiation
to manage disputes.

Comparison of the villages in the Villa Alta marketplace region allows discussion of questions ethnographers have raised about the roles of colonialism, urbanization, capitalist development, and bureaucratic expansion in the development of peasant communities.[3] As corporate communities exposed to external forces, many of which have come to the fore in the past ten years, these villages have both more in common and less in common with each other than the ethnographic literature on Mesoamerican communities would suggest. The villagers vary from the peasant "mean," that is, from the characteristics commonly attributed to peasants involved in a civil-religious organization, mainly as a result of the way they mediate between the numerous dualisms of village life. Both they and the scholars of peasant life have realized that these dualisms are at work in peasant villages. The Villa Alta villagers have used their mediating mechanisms to negotiate various combinations of local, regional, and urban life.

Greenberg (1981, p. 21) characterized the peasant communities of Oaxaca as caught between the limits of local conditions and the demands of larger political-economic systems averse to local concerns. Mediating this dilemma, Greenberg said, are the mechanisms of "closed corporate organization, the fiesta complex, and egalitarian ideologies." I have referred to such mediating mechanisms in Villa Alta as civil-religious organization, regional market systems, the fiesta system, and the principle of the village.

Colonialism contributed to the nucleation of peasant communities (Nader 1969b) and their political-religious organization as independent, self-governing, mostly self-reliant communities marginal to the characteristics of urban development (Wolf 1955, 1957). The independence and the economic and cultural marginality of the peasant communities became a by-product of larger, pyramiding political-economic systems. Both the larger marketplaces and the centralized state authority depended on cooperative and cheap peasant labor to extract gold and cochineal as both capital and tribute. Similarly, the competitive capitalist enterprise that followed colonialism depends on cheap peasant labor and products (Frank 1967, 1972). The colonial organization constructed to extract cochineal from Oaxacan villages led to the development of the dendritic market system (Greenberg 1981) and the regional centralization of opportunities for development within administrative-marketplace villages (Kelley 1976).

In Villa Alta cultural differences and the independence attached to the municipio libre protected market and administrative centers from encroachment on their niches by the Indian peasant. Factors contributing to the creation of peasant communities at odds with one another included differences in language; village endogamy; intervillage competition for land, resources, and marketplaces; the right to assert administrative independence; attachment to local customs and religious rituals; and discrimination and exploitation. These communities were unable to assert authority within the institutions of centralization rather than from outside them.

Just as they did at the time of the Conquest (Pérez García 1956), peasant communities continued to deal with external institutions through emissaries. Individual brokers contributed to the distancing between the village, the administrative plazas, and the urban culture, for those who mediated between the village and other socioeconomic systems benefited from this distance. Literate village secretaries and caciques developed their ties to the external world into personal power and wealth. Brokers moved from control over the flow of documents and paperwork into and out of the village to control over the flow of goods and services, replacing runners with roads, escritos with trucks, and books with coffee. Political-legal brokerage became a capitalist enterprise, and wealth joined hands with culture as a source of local stratification.[4]

Within villages, civil-religious hierarchies converted individual and familial surpluses into community resources. Greenberg (1981, p. 2) classified ethnographic models of the functions of village civil-religious organizations in reference to expenditure of personal wealth as leveling, stratifying, expropriation, and redistribution. In reference to the leveling of socioeconomic differences among villagers of Villa Alta, since the 1920s a portion of the wealth extracted from communities through taxes, bribes, and brokerage has been returned as the incomes and expenditures of Villaltecos. In a regional context, these expenditures have been confined to the seat and urban centers where Villaltecos have relocated. Villaltecos take pride in their economic gains and express them through conspicuous consumption.

This process of expropriation and return within a dendritic market structure has, along with cultural differences between Villaltecos and Indian villagers, contributed to stratification in the seat and region. In the seat, civil-religious organization has functioned to contain but not prevent the expression of local economic differences through conspicuous consumption and enriched life-styles. In most Zapotec villages of the region, where surpluses have been extremely scarce, civil-religious hierarchies have inhibited the stratification of village populations to the point that visible differences in patterns of consumption are rare. Taguí best exhibits the leveling effect of civil-religious organization in the Zapotec villages. Thirteen years after religious conversions began, Protestants who did not contribute to Catholic ceremonies and fiestas had accumulated sufficient surplus to purchase cargo-carrying animals. Catholics continued to carry cargo on their backs.

In the district seat, ritualized traditions for fiestas and special occasions, such as deaths, marriages, and coming-of-age parties, have redistributed resources in a way that highlights local economic stratification. The wealthier residents contribute more to local ceremonies, but the scaling of contributions is not progressive. The ethics of individualism and egalitarianism coexist. Merchants and employees ascribe to individualism in relation to economic contributions and egalitarianism in relation to community service. Campesinos must perform community service and are egalitarian in their community participation. For example, in 1973 employees who held birthday lunches for themselves or family members invited only other employees and important local politicians to participate. Campesinos held open celebrations and invited the entire village. In 1984, Villaltecos organized privately funded celebrations only for marriages. Again, campesinos invited the entire village to their homes. Also, employees successfully lobbied for reductions in fiesta taxes (*cuotas*). Rituals of mourning cut across economic differences, all families providing food and drink in their homes to any mourner for a three-day period.

The coexistence of individualism and egalitarianism has contributed to stratification in the district seat by reinforcing the distance between employees, entrepreneurs, and campesinos. Rituals of civil-religious organization have led to redistribution of some resources on ceremonial occasions (family to village and family to family). Fiestas have led Villaltecos who do not grow subsistence crops into the marketplace, where they purchase turkeys, chickens, beans, and other foodstuffs from Zapotec villagers. (In times of economic scarcity, however, these villagers do not vend such items.)

One institution that benefits from all ceremonies is the Catholic church—through expropriation (Harris 1964). Three examples from the marketplace region show the effects of expropriation: the development of individual surpluses in Taguí following Protestant conversions; opposition to the growth of Catholic influence (and to the filling of church coffers) by wealthy progressive merchants, teachers, middle-men, and latifundistas in the district seat; and villager withdrawal from participation in fiestas and Catholic ceremonies during a period of inflation, economic hardship, and political uncertainty. Neither the wealthy nor the poor can afford an active village religious organization and its rituals, but for different reasons.

This study does not have the economic statistics necessary to reach a conclusion about the dominant functions of village civil-religious organization. Nevertheless, it appears that the overlap of the cargo system and capitalist-bureaucratic development in this dendritic marketplace structure has helped to increase stratification both regionally and in the district seat.

Villages of the region exhibit striking differences, although they share forces generated by capitalist development, the market system, civil-religious organization, and state bureaucratic development. The differences are notable, for they exist in the least "developed" villages. These villages have experienced less contact with larger marketplaces and with Oaxaca City than have other district villages and certainly much less contact than the Zapotec villages of the Valley of Oaxaca.

The villages of Lachirioag and Roayaga have converted much smaller portions of their land to coffee cultivation than have other villages of the region. Most of the villages to the north of Villa Alta— Yetzelalag, Camotlán, Reaguí, Temazcalapa, Yatzona, Yetzecovi, Yala-hui, and Taguí—as well as Yaée and Betaza to the south are coffee cultivators and have received assistance from the Comisión del Compra de Café. Of these major coffee-cultivating villages, only Camotlán, Reaguí, and Betaza have political bosses. The villages without political bosses have hosted Villalteco schoolteachers who have acted as political counselors and brokers.

The major coffee-cultivating villages without political bosses— Yetzelalag, Temazcalapa, Yaa, Yatzona, Yetzecovi, Yalahui, Taguí, and Yaée—have experienced wide-scale conversions to Protestantism over the past ten years, whereas those of only limited cultivation—Lachirioag and Roayaga—have not. The major coffee-cultivating villages with political bosses—Betaza and Camotlán—have experienced political change through political division or have united with regional assemblies. Roayaga has experienced neither religious nor political division, although it cultivates some coffee and is aligned with the Amaya family of Villa Alta; it is the district seat's only ally. All the villages of the region have over the past ten years experienced weakened local civil-religious organization and strengthened ties to some external influence: INI, the Protestant church, regional assemblies, or urban villager groups.

Thus, although some villages now strengthen or develop more than one type of external tie, distinguishing characteristics of villages in the region are that coffee-cultivating villages without political bosses generally develop ties to Protestant groups; coffee-cultivating villages with political bosses generally develop or strengthen ties to political groups; villages that cultivate little coffee develop ties to political groups; and Villa Alta, the administrative-economic plaza, strengthens ties only to urban villager groups. Local Catholic organizations have undergone the least change in the villages that grow little coffee and the villages that do grow coffee but have political bosses.

Over the past ten years, the major coffee-cultivating villages have experienced the impact of economic change and state participation more than other marketplace villages. Forced into the regional marketplace by decreased local cultivation of subsistence goods, they have been the hardest hit by inflation and the most vulnerable to broad fluctuations in market prices for both coffee and subsistence goods. They also have experienced the diminution of patron-client, creditor-borrower, producer-middleman ties to Villaltecos. With the entrance into Villa Alta of the Comisión del Compra de Café and the CONASUPO, many villagers have been set free from indebtedness to Villalteco political leaders.

Without surplus or time to spend on local civil-religious organization and without a strong leadership structure to inhibit them, villagers withdraw from the costly local system of duties. They institutionalize this change and their capitalist status by converting to Protestant faiths and building Protestant churches (but not with their own money). Other villagers exposed to the same external influences respond similarly, though less fully. Lachirioag villagers organized under the influence of teachers from INI and urban villagers to oppose local Catholic-oriented leadership. These villagers, along with groups from the cacique-led villages of Reaguí, Betaza, and Camotlán, joined regional political assemblies to oppose forces they identified as responsible for village economic and organizational problems: caciques, Villa Alta, the state, and Protestants. During this time of economic hardship, all villages strengthened or developed regional or urban ties and alliances.

Some peasant villages in Oaxaca and other parts of Mesoamerica have responded to external forces of change, from colonialism to capitalism, by developing internal and intervillage conflicts. Their conflicts have spawned patterns of violence that have lasted for decades (Dennis 1976, Greenberg, 1981, de la Fuente 1949, Nash 1967). In Villa Alta, where there is no strong and accessible state legal system legitimized by villagers, local ties of cooperation and control have weakened and the power of the forces inhibiting the escalation of disputes and the use of violence has diminished. Nevertheless, villages of this region have turned to negotiation rather than violence in the escalation of their disputes.

The use of negotiation rather than violence between village and regional groups is a product of both village civil-religious organization and the dynamics of the dendritic market system. Traditional village conflicts over individualism versus community and over civil-religious organization are now organized by opposed political and religious groups—a very recent organizational change. Villagers today enact conflicts spawned by their oppositions within a social matrix of kinship, friendship, and neighborliness. Political and religious divisions do not overlap with other social schisms, geographical divisions such as barrios, or mutually exclusive endogamous groups. As in the process of conversion in Taguí, Protestant-Catholic divisions exist within generations, extended families, and nuclear families.

Nader (1965) showed how village civil-religious organization inhibits the development of local social schisms by generating ties that cut across groups in Talea, a village in the Villa Alta district. Members of village groups, such as fiesta committees, the band, daily volunteer work forces (*tequíos*), agricultural committees, and even the elected village government, are drawn from families in all parts of this relatively large village. As membership of village groups varies from year to year, Taleanos participate in many groups, moving from one group to another and working in cooperation with different villagers. In this way, ties of cooperation and friendship develop where ties of kinship and compadrazgo may not exist, and from cooperation other forms of exchange may grow.

The principle of crosscutting ties suggests that when individuals in a village belong to more than one group, such as a church committee and the village band, they share the interests of both groups. Should a member of one group enter into a dispute with a member of the other, individuals who belong to both groups have an interest in preventing the escalation of the dispute. Should the dispute escalate into group-based conflict, these individuals must make a choice to ally with one group or the other. By choosing sides, they sever or weaken their ties to the group not chosen. Those who have their feet in both groups are natural third-party mediators, less partial than those who belong to only one of the groups, and more capable of preventing disputes from escalating.

Studies by Koch (1974) of the Jale of New Guinea and by Thoden Van Velsen and Van Wetering (1960) of patrilocal and matrilocal tribal societies showed that effective local mediation is a product of ties that crosscut the geographic and interest groups of a society. In the absence of effective local third parties, disputants may turn to external remedy agents or employ violence or avoidance locally.

Although the effects of community service are diminishing in marketplace villages, political and religious conflicts take place in the context of social forces that support the benefits of negotiated compromise of differences. Elected village authorities and state legal officials do not now provide the impartiality (actual or perceived) necessary for successful mediation or adjudication of escalating disputes. Avoidance of disputes that develop along crosscutting ties within a small village is nearly impossible over an extended period of time. Since the costs of violence are high where differences cut across ties of kinship and reciprocity, negotiation through extant local channels of communication—village networks of kinship, friendship, and neighborliness—is the most viable alternative.

Negotiation is a process in which information is exchanged between differing parties as a mode of argument and persuasion. It is foremost a creative process into which disputants may introduce political and economic power to forge a relationship that may endure over time. In this process differences of principle and value may be put aside, debated, or bargained. What keeps negotiation going is the desire shared by disputants to continue their relationship or forge a new one without severing ties of communication. They may be motivated by the prospect of mutual benefit or the spectre of mutual loss should communication break down.

Disputes among Zapotec villagers progress from political and religious conflicts to specific disputes that engage local divisions. Villagers may then escalate their disputes into Protestant and regional assemblies. Although both assemblies have funds for formal legal action, most escalated disputes move through regional assemblies and village groups into urban channels. There regional and village-state oppositions are expressed by both groups through the written word. In their publications, Protestant and regional assemblies disseminate accounts of disputes (and their specific resolutions) among member groups throughout the marketplace region. Villagers also disseminate and retrieve information through networks and groups of urban villagers. Regional organizations function in negotiations to gather, interpret, condense, and disseminate information. Pooling of resources on a regional basis through village participation in assemblies provides organization and leadership for local negotiating teams, political and religious. Negotiations that are now both regional and local are contained by long-contested cultural, historical, and economic conflicts expressed in oppositions, such as village versus state, village versus

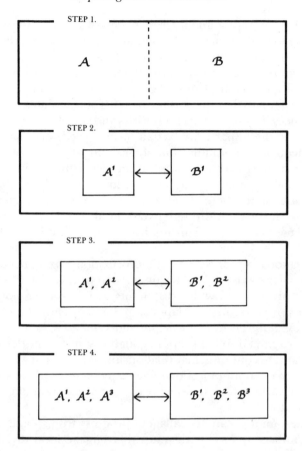

church, and Zapotec versus Spanish. Protestant and regional assemblies share and develop further the village versus state and Zapotec versus Spanish oppositions.

The social structure in which disputes in the village of Villa Alta expand and reach a resolution can be depicted in segments representing opponents in the disputes (see Figure 3).[5] Conflicts between village divisions (A and B), as well as ties of kinship, cooperation, and neighborliness that cut across these divisions, provide the social context for disputing (step 1). As a conflict between two individuals enters into the public arena and becomes a dispute, information about the dispute first spreads through personal communication networks and among allied kin (A^1 and B^1) of the disputants (step 2). These networks may or may not overlap with political or religious divisions.

Disputants may then define their differences in terms of village divisions, or, in some cases, members of the divisions may adopt the

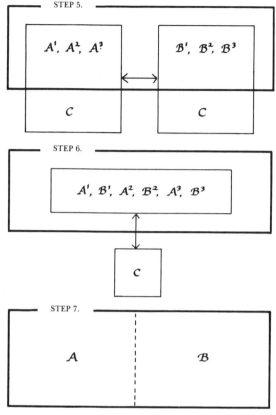

Figure 3. The Village.

dispute as an issue related to villagewide conflicts. That may happen
under the following circumstances: when disputants are uncertain
about rights and duties in their relationships; when the dispute is over
a political or religious issue or between villagers who define their
relationship in terms of local divisions; or when there is a general
atmosphere of uncertainty, in which case villagers may use the dispute
to generate debate and negotiation over larger conflicts. At this point,
the dispute leads to the organization of villagers by their political and
religious alliances (step 3). Although before the dispute villagers related to one another as kin or committee members they now relate as
members of opposed village groups (A^2 and B^2).

The disputants are now defined in terms of regional and larger
oppositions, such as church versus village and village versus state.
Negotiations over villagewide conflicts begin across local divisions.
Villagers assume their roles in the dispute as representatives of ties to

external institutions, fighters for local control, challengers of caciques, opponents of capitalist development, and so on. At this point villagers also may activate ties to external groups symbolizing local oppositions. Opposed village groups or segments may unite with like segments in the region. Zapotec village groups may escalate the dispute into allied regional assemblies, Protestant assemblies, and political parties that play informational, organizational, and economic roles in the disputing process. In the district seat, economic and occupational stratification of the resident and urban population provides examples sufficient to integrate changes into village legal processes without forming alliances with regional groups. This stratification has produced a political class of Villaltecos with the time and resources to provide local leadership that organizes opposition disputing or negotiating teams. Escalating disputes bypass the region and enter into urban networks and groups.

As villagers fill out the symbolic cast of participants in order to create from the dispute a comprehensive ordering of oppositions, they disseminate information among allied urban villagers who enter into the disputing process (step 4), broadening the net of social order through their own relationships to the external world (A^3 and B^3). At this point, disputants draw on village communication networks to order relationships among individuals and groups representing external institutions with possible links to village society.

The next step (5) brings into the dispute an opponent (C) that is shared by the groups in conflict. Such an opponent may already be symbolized by some of the disputants, or villagers may deliberately introduce the opponent into the dispute. The opponent represents a common threat to the village. For politically divided villages the opponent may be Protestants; for religiously divided villages it may be the state, Villaltecos, or caciques; for Villaltecos it may be Protestants, the state, regional assemblies, or other Zapotec coalitions.

Disputants then contain the escalated dispute by reaching a compromise on the conditions under which they will unify to oppose the external threat (step 6). The compromise involves agreement on definitions of local roles and village relationships to external institutions. This agreement may be temporary, may produce a change in the relative power of village segments, or may be a return to the coexistence that was present prior to the dispute (step 7).[6] Through this process the village expands to include urban villagers and external groups as participants in its local processes of dispute settlement, while also demarcating and maintaining the boundaries between local and external authority.

Although villagers may not resolve their conflicts decisively through this process of dispute escalation, they do vent their spleens, clarify uncertainties, renew old ties and alliances (especially to urbanites), and place what they consider threats to their lives in the proper places. As the tensions of local conflicts and those associated with disorder increase, the process of first escalating disputes and then simplifying them releases and reduces the tensions—until they again accumulate in the natural process of events.[7]

As we saw in chapters 2 and 4, the 1984 disputes in Villa Alta arose in the context of a local conflict (step 1). They escalated through networks of kin, compadres, neighbors, friends, and co-workers (step 2). The disputes were then organized for the process of negotiation as members of political groups and their leaders reinterpreted them in the context of villagewide conflicts (step 3). These conflicts over relationships to external groups then led to the inclusion of individuals who symbolized these groups and their specific relationships to them (step 4).

At this point, as illustrated in chapter 4, the escalating disputes included the village court, the district court, the Catholic church, offices of state bureaucracies, and urban villagers. Villaltecos then incorporated, evaluated, and located the components of the village and the ties that disseminated from it into the region, state, and nation. To both maintain and contain dispute escalation and intergroup negotiations, and to prioritize systems of authority (village, state, church, region), the villagers then introduced an authority-based opposition (step 5) which Progressives and Caleros evaluated similarly—the Zapotec villages (represented by coalitions of villagers, conspiracies, and regional assemblies). The Villaltecos then used this common opponent to move closer together and to strike a compromise (step 6).[8]

The recognition of external threats is a component of the contemporary viewpoint of marketplace villagers as they consider their roles in the region, state, and nation. The recognition of problems real and potential associated with Mexico's economic crisis integrates the threat of instability into daily decision-making. Daily discussions of the crisis include concern over the stability of the state and national governments, the role of the United States in Mexican domestic policy, and the future ability of villagers to meet their daily needs. Regional assemblies form to manage what they perceive as several threats to their concept of the village. As threats to boundaries, ongoing processes, and cohesion of the village, they identify Protestantism and associated village divisions, caciques, and the national political party PRI. The extended village of Villa Alta identifies as threats both regional assem-

blies and Protestantism—regional assemblies as a challenge to the
district seat status of Villa Alta and Protestantism as a challenge to
village civil processes.

Adams (1975, p. 211) identified external pressure on a society as a
force of centralization that demands internal coordination. Naroll and
Divale (1976) noted the same phenomenon in their study of structural
adaptation in patrilocal societies that migrated to new territories.
Thoden Van Velsen and Van Wetering (1960) noted that matrilocal
rules of residency distributed male kin across different settlements.
Crosscutting ties then developed among groups that intermarried.
Internal third-party mediators were able to settle disputes among these
groups. Matrilocal societies tended to settle their disputes peacefully
and to experience internal cohesiveness. Patrilocal societies, in which
male kin were not dispersed, lacked third-party mediators and tended
to use violence to manage disputes.

Naroll and Divale (1976) found that when patrilocal societies migrated to new territories and faced threats from groups already residing in these territories, they eventually became matrilocal. In the face
of external threats, patrilocal societies experienced structural change
in the direction of rules of marital residency that facilitated coordination among their settlements, the development of third parties to
manage disputes across settlements, and greater internal cohesion.

Escalating disputes in Villa Alta follow the cyclical pattern detailed
by Gulliver (1979) for the process of negotiation. Teams move together
and move apart (fusion and fission) while at the same time exchanging
information through which they can forge a compromise. Once all
components of the village social system are represented in a dispute,
the "common threat" opposition both forces and offers a compromise
that confirms the authority of villagers in the disputing process. At this
point villagers may agree upon the status of an external component,
new element, or local irritant and place it in a context of local relationships—within, on the margin, or outside of village life.

In negotiations villagers do not symbolize abstract forces, such as
capitalism, the Catholic church, bureaucratic development, and Zapotec villagers. Rather, villagers represent the specific relationships to
these forces that they have established in the historical development of
the seat. For example, the mero cacique David Mendiolea represents
the specific relationship he has established between the capitalist economy and village politics, while the mero cacique Raul Torres represents
specific relationships among the Catholic church, state bureaucracies,
cash-cropping, patronage, and local leadership.

Villaltecos retain the personal and familiar quality of their escalated
disputes. They are disputing about specific and immediate problems to

seek management and compromises that are accessible to all villagers. As they include representatives of the district court, the Catholic church, and the technical school in their disputes, they personalize such institutions by integrating them into the familiar context of local historical conflicts and tensions between generations, families, and villages.

Villages of the region have been more open economically than politically. Though they are now open politically, too, it is in a way that preserves the corporate nature of village life while at the same time expanding village social systems to include groups of the region, the state capital, and Mexico City. Through negotiated compromises, villagers are incorporating into their communities groups from which they have been excluded in an effort to regulate the effects of their own marginality.[9]

Negotiation is a creative process with a predictable conclusion only within the range of relationships that are acceptable to both teams. While exposed to the forces of various structures of local, regional, and state socioeconomic systems, villagers have given these forces and institutions names and identities. They have assumed authority over them in rendering them manipulable in the context of village histories, relationships, conflicts, and ideologies. As in a process of invention (White 1949), each village has created its own identities and relationships among the various elements of village life.

The negotiation of compromises among the opposition forces of village life has produced variations across the villages of Villa Alta's marketplace region within the context of relatively homogeneous lifestyles. Two general types of social systems are emerging, one with a regional component (Zapotec) and the other not regional but urban (Villalteco), in which urban migrants play influential roles in village politics, governance, and economy. Just where an individual village falls along a regional-urban continuum corresponds to its level of stratification. The maize growers of Lachirioag, the coffee cultivators of Temazcalapa, the Witnesses of Taguí, and the brokers of Villa Alta meet today in new "marketplaces" where the products are information and society. They return to their municipios libres to create their own social systems. As villagers combine what they have in common with the specific characteristics of each village, they preserve and elaborate the differences that were forged in past negotiations.

Village legal systems are truly integrative, combining new components of village life with past village identities and relationships. Through local legal processes villagers are casting a wide intellectual net to create new local social orders. The State encapsulates the village geographically and institutionally as it brings all the political units of

Oaxaca under its administration. But in the district of Villa Alta, the state is not a force of centralization socially, processually, or ideologically. While the state presence is indeed growing materially and symbolically through development projects and buildings, internal village forces of centralization do not direct social, political, and legal development through state channels of centralization. Villagers cannot use disputes to explore new relationships when they become subject to the formal application of state legal codes. The villages of Villa Alta are responding to the forces of centralization through the village rather than the state. The village provides flexible and uncodified tradition; open legal forums; and the principles, processes, and rationales by which villagers develop alternative associations and hierarchies for local, regional, and state groups and institutions. Through the creative participatory processes of the village, villagers are able to use local disputes and legal processes to construct and order intergroup relations.[10]

The study of village law as it varies across quite similar communities provides a somewhat controlled research setting that lends itself to such questions as how the functions of law vary or coincide in the presence of definable social, cultural, and economic differences. The study of variations in law within a region of similar communities introduces the interesting factor that both the comparative researcher and the people under study may be aware of the definable differences that characterize their communities. In such situations, the social, cultural, and economic differences that distinguish neighbors exist not only as social forces but also as cultural materials that the researcher and the community alike can use in the process of social analysis.

Villaltecos use village law as an analytic system. Through legal processes, they personalize political projects and preferences, the church and its judgments, the challenges and threats they perceive in their neighbors, the harms of immorality and overindulgence, the acceptable limits of avarice and ambition, and the generosity and cooperation that hold their societies together. As villagers in the Valley of Oaxaca weave clothes and those on the coast paint and carve masks, Villaltecos weave yarns and construct identities out of daily lives and social relationships.

Village law is symmetrical. Because village law exists only in social relationships and in memory, Villalteco legal identities are confined to legal processes. That is one reason why Villaltecos can manage or resolve disputes by turning them into social resources—the building blocks of social order. Villaltecos limit their legal processes to certain times and particular goals. They can collectively raise and lower the curtain on legal processes. The identities villagers assume or are given in disputing processes fall dormant when villagers recognize that the dispute is over—or until the next dispute begins. In Villa Alta the seminarian is "not a seminarian" only when he enters into a dispute with the padre, and the padre is a "half-father" only when he enters into a dispute with the Progressives.

The punishments of village law—primarily the limiting of access to political statuses and influence—are confined to legal processes. Villagers who have difficulty managing their problems in acceptable ways may participate in disputes, but if their disputing function is unclear, they enter at the risk of having their problems resurrected and retold as village lore. As a result, while village law functions to order social identities and systems, it does not interfere with the ongoing processes of village life and relationships that maintain families, economies, and other activities.

Village law derives elasticity from its symmetry. Villaltecos can create dispute and morality tales as they attempt to impose disputing identities on each other, because they also have the power to remove these identities. In other words, they are conscious of the functions of law and create rules that confine the processes of developing dispute information to the goal of creating and evaluating social relationships.

Because of its symmetry and elasticity, village law is integrative. In disputing processes individuals represent groups, and through the creation of individual identities Villaltecos evaluate group relationships. Once the end point of creating a social pattern or order is reached, the identities created for individuals as symbols of group-based relationships dissolve. In the disputing processes of the extended village, individuals may play negatively valued roles in gossip without fear of retribution. But when Villaltecos tie their imposition of negative identities of fellow villagers to physical force through apprehension and jailing, those who use force lose political power and status.

Villaltecos create a nonpunitive system of law that turns problems into social resources. In recognizing the common plight of human frailty Villaltecos use problem-solving as a means of exploring and ordering the world through social imagination. The benefits of village law are knowledge and a sense of social order and social authority. By participating in village law, the villagers bring the world to their village, render it accessible and human, and control their fears when the world seems unpredictable and out of control.

One lesson to be learned from the study of law in Villa Alta is that when people treat disputing as an expressive path to knowledge, as a social adventure, law can solve problems and expand personal and social boundaries. Certainly, all the problems of the larger world exist in Villa Alta—economic inequality, discrimination, uncured illness, hunger, anger, envy, and fear. Yet all villagers have access to village legal processes. As they participate in disputes, they reap rewards inherent in social ties.

During my research in Villa Alta I led two lives, one in my daily interactions and the other in the imaginations of Villaltecos. I learned that as I sat at my desk typing field notes, conducted an interview, or worked on a fiesta committee, I was not only a thirty-five-year-old North American anthropologist but also a white-haired seventy-year-old man, a spy for the Taleanos, an employee of the Mexican government, a friend of the United States president. My identities varied as village life moved from fiesta to fiesta, from planting to harvest, and from conflict to dispute. Yet I was welcomed into village life because I performed the duties of a local citizen.

Living so many lives and listening as the identities of other villagers also assumed various hues in the conversations of Villaltecos, I found that it was impossible to view my neighbors as passive participants in the development of their villages. Their litigiousness, born of reciprocity and rewarded by an integrative and informal legal system, was serving them well. Villaltecos gave me the rare opportunity to watch the past—conquest, reform, revolution, and institutionalization—merge with the present and the future in the very moment when Villaltecos articulated them. In the Villa Alta marketplace region, those who keep the peace and turn adversity into society are indeed the people.

APPENDIX

THE OAXACA STATE LEGAL SYSTEM OF APPEALS

This description of the official state legal system of Oaxaca explains the judicial, penal, and investigative roles of persons who officially represent the state in the village, the judicial district, and the state capital. It also covers the relationships among these positions that are prescribed in state law.

The blueprint for the official judicial structure in the district and the village is established in the state capital with a division of legal labors between the state Tribunal Superior, or Superior Court, and the office of the *procurador general*, or state attorney general. The Tribunal Superior is responsible for judicial review and sentencing, and the office of the procurador general is responsible for investigations, apprehensions, and representation of the state in criminal cases. These offices are represented by appointed subordinates on the district level and elected subordinates on the village level.

This description is concerned primarily with the responsibilities of persons who work in and are responsible to the Tribunal Superior and the procurador general and of certain auxiliary offices that fall under their jurisdictions in the processing of cases on the district level. The organization of positions through which disputes arising among residents of the region of Oaxaca City are processed varies from that found in the satellite districts of the state. However, I am not here concerned with urban disputes and do not delve into the organization of dispute settlement in the local urban legal bureaucracy.

At no point in the processing of a case in the state judicial system does the defendant receive a jury trial. All decisions of guilt and innocence are made by elected officials on the village level and appointed officials on the district and state levels. Case investigations are conducted primarily through on-site inspections by judicial officials and through the taking of testimony of witnesses. In general, both the district and state judicial officials assume a passive role in the investigation of criminal acts. The responsibility for the presentation of evidence and witnesses to back up accusations generally falls to the plaintiff in a criminal case. All communications among officials on the three judicial levels are through telegrams and correspondence carried in the mail or by runners.

A case of homicide from the district of Villa Alta is presented at the end of this appendix to illustrate relationships and roles in the official system.

INVESTIGATION AND PROSECUTION

The Procuradoria

The Procuradoria, a two-story building in Oaxaca City, houses the office of the procurador general. The procurador is appointed by the governor of Oaxaca and holds jurisdiction over the Oaxaca-based sub-procuradores, who are also appointed by the governor. The procurador names directors of his administrative offices as well as his district and regional counterparts, the *agentes de ministerio público auxiliares, adscritos* (appointed), and *investigadores*. He also has jurisdiction over the offices of the Dirección de Averiguaciones y Consignaciones (Investigations and Consignments) and the Dirección de Control de Procesos (Office of Case Control). The state judicial police and the following offices fall under the jurisdiction of the procurador: control, *investigaciones, prestaciones* (loans), *aprehensiones*, and *investigaciones inmediatos o de emergencia*.

In district cases that have not spread to include the Tribunal Superior:

1. The procurador general reviews recommendations of the district ministerio público adscrito before they are sent to the district judge or after they are overturned by the district judge. The ministerio público, at his discretion, requests the aid of the procurador in formulating these decisions, including accusations and recommendations for sentencing.

2. District judicial authorities must submit investigations that do not result in accusations to the procurador. They must also submit investigations that do not result in the issuance of an act of formal imprisonment and cases in which the information obtained in investigations does not warrant the actions taken by judicial authorities.

3. The ministerio público must submit to the procurador a copy of his account of acts and investigations conducted and issued in a case.

4. The procurador general may order the judicial and special police to aid the ministerio público in case investigations.

5. The procurador general assigns the ministerios públicos to judicial districts and reprimands those whose guilt has been demonstrated in the infractions of penal, civil, or procedural codes.

The *Ministerio Público*

The ministerio público is the representative of the procurador general in district penal affairs. Each *cabecera*, or district seat, hosts a ministerio público adscrito and a secretario (secretary) to the ministerio público.

These salaried agents of the procurador hold jurisdiction over all villages in their assigned district. Investigations that are appealed by villages to district judicial agencies are assigned initially to the ministerio público. On appeal of a village case to the district, parties to the case and the village investigation are consigned to the ministerio público. The secretario performs the functions of the ministerio público when he is absent and shares his investigative and administrative duties when he is present.

District ministerios públicos generally have no formal legal training. They gain a knowledge of law and legal procedure through apprenticeships, primarily as secretarios. They obtain their positions through political contacts.

Article 1 of the Ley Orgánica (Organic Regulations) del Ministerio Público states:

> The *ministerio público*, as representative of the social interests in justice, is the institution indivisible and of good faith, which holds the responsibility to keep watch over lawfulness as one of the principal rectors of social communion, to contribute to the maintenance of the established legal order, to exercise penal action demanding the reparation of damage, to look after the correct application of the standards of criminal prudence, and to protect collective and individual interests against all arbitrariness.

Article 2 of the code states that the ministerio público shall carry out the above functions through the following activities:

1. Conducting an *averiguación previa,* or investigation, into possible infractions that come to his knowledge. The purposes of the investigation are to prove the body of the crime and establish the probable responsibility of the accused.

2. Exercising penal action and reparation of damage.

3. Maintaining vigilance over lawfulness as one of the principal rectors of social communion.

The ministerio público may initiate the averiguación previa on the basis of his own knowledge of the crime (*de oficio*), or may initiate an investigation through the statement of a plaintiff—an individual, group, or local court. In the averiguación previa:

1. The ministerio público takes the testimony of the plaintiff, the witnesses, and the accused. He must ratify the testimony rendered by parties before village authorities in appealed cases. He may expand on the testimony of parties by asking them further questions. All the testimony is recorded by the ministerio público or his secretary at a typewriter. Once the ministerio público has recorded the testimony of a party, he must read the testimony back to the party. The party may then decide whether or not to verify the testimony as his own by signing his name to the record or, if illiterate, by placing his fingerprints on the record.

2. The ministerio público may take necessary steps to aid the victims of a crime and ensure their security.

3. The ministerio público must describe the physical condition of parties who are victims of the crime. He must also describe the nature of the crime and the damage to property or persons resulting from it. He may gather descriptive information through testimony or through conducting an on-site inspection. He may conduct inspections himself or authorize a *perito,* an individual qualified to assess the nature of the damage, to conduct the inspection for him and submit a written assessment. While investigating a crime, the ministerio público may request the aid of the Oaxaca judicial police and the state criminal

laboratory. He also has access to the records and documents of other governmental institutions.

4. To clarify contradictions he discovers in court testimony, the ministerio público may initiate the *careo*, a formal debate between parties.

5. In cases involving the death of a party, the ministerio público is responsible for ordering an autopsy, burial, and the issuance of a death certificate. If he determines that a death does not involve the commission of a crime, he must ask the permission of the procurador general to turn the responsibility of the autopsy over to interested parties. Even if the death does not involve the commission of a crime, the ministerio público or a subordinate must issue orders for burial as well as the death certificate.

6. If the ministerio público determines that, according to state law, a crime has been committed and a specific individual has committed the crime, he must formulate his accusations and ask the district judge to issue an order of apprehension against the accused.

7. The ministerio público must send the original and one copy of all steps in his investigation to the district judge, send one copy within twenty-four hours to the procurador general, and retain one copy for the archives of his own office.

Once the ministerio público can substantiate the commission of a crime and the probable responsibility of an accused, he consigns the averiguación previa to the district court. Once he has consigned the case:

1. He may be present in all investigative acts of the district judge.

2. He must receive a copy of all acts issued by the district judge and must send a copy of these acts to the procurador general. He must also retain a copy of all his own formulations in response to the judge's actions and send a copy of them to the procurador general.

3. He must receive from the district judge all formulations of conclusions in the case. He must formulate his recommendations for judicial action and send them to the judge, supporting his recommendations by citing legal codes. He must also ask for reparation of damage caused by the crime.

4. He must visit parties detained in the case to maintain an account of their conditions and any complaints they may wish to express. He must notify the procurador general of their condition and complaints.

5. He must keep watch over the actions of the district judge and help maintain conformity of his actions with the laws of the state.

6. He must not detain any party for more than three days without the issuance of an act of formal imprisonment by the district judge.

The Dirección de Control de Procesos

The Dirección de Control de Procesos performs much of the paperwork assigned to the procurador general through his responsibility for oversight of the district ministerios públicos. This office also performs other mediatory functions with law enforcement agents under the procurador's jurisdiction. Copies of acts issued by the district judges and recommendations issued by the ministerios públicos originally go to the Dirección de Control. This office also keeps watch over the steps taken by ministerios públicos in the development of cases to ensure that their investigations unfold in accordance with state legal procedure. It notifies the procurador general of any infractions. If necessary it may assign additional personnel to a district investigation. It submits to the procurador an annual statistical report on cases that have been processed by the district courts.

The *Síndico Procurador*

Each *municipio,* a residential unit of 2,000 or more inhabitants, must elect a *síndico procurador* who, within the state legal system, is the local substitute and auxiliary agent of the ministerio público. Municipal governments with more than ten elected members may elect two síndicos. Síndicos serve a two-year term. To be eligible for any elected position in municipal government a villager must be a Mexican citizen eighteen years of age or older, must have lived in the municipio for one year or be a native of the municipio, must be present on election day, and must make an "honest living." According to the 1971 Ley Orgánica de Ayuntamientos del Estado de Oaxaca, women may vote in municipal matters and be elected to municipal office.

According to state law, the nonsalaried síndico may exercise the functions on the local level that the ministerio público is assigned on the district level. In general, the village síndico conducts the *primeras diligencias,* the initial investigations of disputes. These investigations, with the aid of peritos and local police, may include all the steps prescribed for the ministerio público in case investigations.

In disputes that expand to include state judicial agencies, the primary role of the síndico is to take the testimony of witnesses and to describe the nature of the crime and the damage it caused. After the dispute is appealed to the ministerio público, he may request that the síndico accumulate additional information on the dispute. When a party to a dispute takes his case directly to the ministerio público, bypassing the municipio, or if the ministerio público initiates the investigation without a formal complaint, the ministerio público may request that the síndico perform the primeras diligencias after case initiation on the district level.

The *Agente Municipal* and the *Agente de Policía*

Agencias, or political residential units of less than 2,000 inhabitants, elect an *agente municipal* in place of a *presidente* and *alcalde.* Units of fewer than 200 inhabitants elect an *agente de policía.* According to state municipal law, the legal role of the nonsalaried agente is to give an account to the municipal authorities who hold jurisdiction over the agencia of any offense or of any offender of the public order who appears in the agencia. The municipal síndico then treats the offense or the offender or both in the same way he would treat similar elements in his own municipio. The agente, with the aid of agencia police, must also apprehend any offender and place him or her at the disposition of the municipio. The agente municipal and the agente de policía generally act according to local custom rather than state law in administrative and penal affairs.

INVESTIGATION AND JUDGMENT

The Tribunal Superior del Estado

The presidente of the Tribunal Superior del Estado de Oaxaca holds administrative jurisdiction over state district courts as well as other state judicial agencies. He maintains ultimate responsibility in appointing district judges, secretaries, and executors and in assigning them to district courts. During his tenure the presidente sets the direction of law in Oaxaca and may assume the task of revising state legal codes. He is appointed by the governor for a six-year tenure and is generally drawn from the ranks of Oaxaca lawyers.

The six appointed *magistrados* of the Tribunal Superior review the appealed decisions of district judges. They do not conduct or order additional investigations into an appealed case. They base their decisions on case summaries submitted to the Tribunal Superior by the district judges. Magistrados generally uphold the district judge in an appealed case in the areas of determination of commission of a crime and responsibility. They generally modify the sentence of a district judge by imposing a lighter sentence.

The *juez mixto de primera instancia,* or district judge, is appointed to his position by the presidente of the Tribunal Superior. He is generally formally trained in Mexican law, although formal training is not a prerequisite. Borja Osorno (1969) in his discussion of the penal process in Mexico explains the official role of the district judge (my translation):

1. Once [the judge] has been invested with the penal action, that is to say, with the demand to issue a decision concerning a specified criminal act, he is obligated to prepare the legal brief to its conclusion [that is, to the sentence], without attributing any efficacy to fortuitous acts of withdrawal from the lawsuit.

2. [The judge] must omit, in the formation of material of cognition, the conduct of the parties in the lawsuit. In effect, during the court proceedings, his investigation of the material of cognition is perfectly free [he may, at his discretion, call witnesses, order statements based on practical knowledge, inspections, and other forms of verification and proof]; and, during the argument, even if he attributes principal importance to the investigations of the parties, he is equally free. Thus he may officially order statements based on practical knowledge; he may officially order the inspection of places; in general, he may officially order new means of gathering evidence. Since in his search for the truth the penal judge may not be subject to any limitation, no importance is given to the impulse of a party.

3. [The judge] must, in the decision, omit investigations of the parties,

being able to pronounce punishment even in the event of demand of absolution by the ministerio público, and be able to absolve even in the event of confession of the accused or a request of a sentence against him.

When the ministerio público assigns a case to the district judge:

1. The district judge notifies the presidente of the Tribunal Superior of his initiation of the case.

2. The district judge ratifies parties to the case in their testimony that has been offered in the primeras diligencias and the averiguación previa. He may expand on their testimony through direct questioning.

3. The district judge may conduct additional investigations into the nature of the crime and the damage caused by it. In these investigations he may use peritos, doctors, village court officials, and police, as well as the police of the district seat.

4. The district judge, if he determines that it is appropriate on the basis of the case investigation, may order the apprehension of the accused. The ministerio público then sends the order of apprehension to the procurador general, who orders its activation.

5. The district judge, if he deems it fit in accordance with state law, may order the formal imprisonment of an accused.

6. With an accused present, the district judge takes his or her declaración preparatoria, or his or her initial declaration after consignment of the case, to the district court.

7. Once parties to the case have ratified and expanded on their previous testimony, the district judge must place them in a *careo*, or debate. Careos consist of two parties only. The judge reads contradictions in their testimony to the parties and asks them to discuss the contradictions in his presence.

8. The district judge must notify the ministerio público of all acts he formulates in the processing of a case.

9. Once the district judge formulates his conclusions, he must submit them to the ministerio público for comments. The ministerio público may appeal any acts formulated by the district judge.

10. Once the ministerio público consigns a case to the district judge, the judge must notify parties to testify within twenty-four hours of the consignment.

11. The district judge must provide an interpreter for all parties who cannot speak or understand Spanish.

12. The district judge must inform the accused that he may name a defender, allow him to name witnesses whom he may call in his favor, determine whether the accused has penal antecedents, allow witnesses to testify to the character of the accused, and determine the nature of the accused's conduct while imprisoned.

13. The district judge sends all autopsy reports to *médicas legistas* (medical examiners) assigned to the Tribunal Superior, for their opinion.

14. The district judge may suspend a case at the request of the plaintiff or when he cannot obtain the physical presence of parties necessary to provide additional evidence. A suspended case is entered into the court archives.

15. The district judge is responsible for arranging for the transfer of prisoners when it is either requested by the prisoner or mandated by the judge.

The *Secretario* and *Ejecutor*

The salaried secretario to the juez mixto de primera instancia performs the functions of the judge when the judge is absent and assists him when he is present. The secretario has no formal legal training. Secretarios are generally drawn from the ranks of court *ejecutores* (expediters), who also function as secretarios, and are appointed on the basis of influence rather than technical capability. Secretarios and ejecutores may exercise only the administrative and investigative authority assigned to them by the judge or that which falls to them in the judge's absence. When a judge is present the secretario and ejecutor are generally responsible for taking and recording testimony and preparing copies of recorded testimony and acts. They are responsible for keeping court financial records as well as case records. The secretario or ejecutor must also prepare copies of case records for the court archives and maintain the order of the archives. They act as witnesses to penal and civil matters conducted in the court offices.

The *Registrar Civil*

The functions of the salaried *registrar civil* may be performed by either the judge or an appointed *registrar*. The registrar keeps records of births, marriages, and deaths; performs civil marriage ceremonies; and may assist in the preparation of civil documents. He may not perform any penal or judicial functions.

Interpreters and Defenders

Interpreters are generally drawn from district villagers and assigned to individual cases. They are paid on a piece-rate basis. Defenders may be either licensed lawyers from Oaxaca City or district villagers who are literate and familiar with state penal processes. Defenders arrange remuneration for their services with individual clients.

The *Juez Tercero de lo Penal*

The *juez tercero* (third judge) serves as an aide to the district judge in matters involving either investigative action in Oaxaca City or the delivery of notifications in the city. He is responsible for delivering notifications to and gathering information from district prisoners in the state penitentiary.

The *Tesorero*

The *tesorero*, or treasurer, is not an official of the district court but is the treasurer of the government of the district seat. His role in district affairs centers on the maintenance of prisoners in the jail through collecting payments from village governments. Payments are assessed on the basis of population size. The treasurer is not paid for his services.

Cabecera Police

Prisoners in the district jails are guarded by the district seat police force. A local citizen is assigned the *cargo* of keeper of the jail keys. Ultimate responsibility for district prisoners falls on a *regidor*, or director, of the district seat police force. Neither the regidor nor the local police are paid for their services.

All village police fall under the jurisdiction of village governments. Each municipio and agencia maintains a jail under the vigilance of local police. Local police are also responsible for apprehensions of prisoners mandated by the síndico. They also serve as messengers in delivering notices from the síndico to parties to a dispute. They are expected to aid judicial police in case investigations. They are not paid for their services.

The *Presidente Municipal*

The *presidente* of a village, an elected official, may assume the functions of the síndico or alcalde or perform these functions in tandem with the elected court officials. The presidente is generally instrumental in the settlement of administrative and political disputes. He is not paid for his services.

Peritos

Peritos, on the district level, are villagers called on to offer expert advice in the assessment of damages caused by a crime. They may, at the request of the ministerio público, conduct on-site inspections. Peritos who assess physical injuries are generally paramedics trained through correspondence courses. Peritos are also called on to perform autopsies. They are paid either by the courts on a piece-rate basis or by local governments.

CHECKS AND BALANCES

On the district level of the state judicial system, the offices of the ministerio público and the juez mixto de primera instancia constitute a system of checks and balances. The ministerio público and the judge maintain vigilance over each other's actions and, through correspondence, push for the completion of steps dictated by penal procedure.

The notification system among the local, district, and state judicial institutions also motivates the processual and timely enactment of judicial investigations. State agencies maintain a bureaucratic watch over their subordinate institutions and, on the basis of information these subordinates provide, maintain both the logic and the legality of the judicial bureaucracies.

Internal regulation is necessary in the state judicial system, for in practice most of the processual steps performed by judicial officials take place behind closed doors. Audiences held by the district judge are not open to the public. The delivery and recording of testimony is also closed to public view. Lawyers do not have free access to case information and may examine the testimony of their clients only by permission of the judge.

The onus of responsibility for public regulation of the judicial bureaucracy falls on the shoulders of the participants in criminal cases. The local courts and the parties to a case are the only public individuals who have access to empirical knowledge of the workings of the court system. On both the district and the state levels, only the parties, by being subjects of the courts, develop inside knowledge of the operation of the judicial bureaucracy. Local court officials do not have access to information up the line of appeals. The knowledge parties develop of the judicial bureaucracy by participating in it is useless in regulating the bureaucracy unless it is also coupled with a knowledge of written legal and administrative codes.

For the illiterate majority of the district of Villa Alta, state law is inaccessible. Copies of the state codes may be bought at the offices of the Periódico Oficial del Gobierno del Estado de Oaxaca, but copies of the up-to-date penal codes regulating the actions of district and state agencies are not available in these offices, even for judicial personnel. On the local level, knowledge of the actions of state judicial personnel and the operation of judicial bureaucracies is passed by word of mouth. For the average villager it is difficult to distinguish between practice and legality.

Parties to a case may demand *amparo,* or the protection by the state judiciary from actions by district judicial officials. The demand of amparo is processed by the *juez del distrito* (judge of the district) in Oaxaca City. In the written demand, the party, now the plaintiff, accuses judicial officials of abuses of their authority. These officials must submit case documents to the judgment of the juez del distrito. On demand of amparo, a party is freed from prosecution pending the judgment from Oaxaca City. The punishment of judicial officials guilty of abuse of authority is administrative rather than penal.

One clause in the state law attempts to reconstitute a balance among disputants: the reparation of damage clause. The enforcement of this clause is a primary responsibility of the ministerio público. In no case I know of in the Villa Alta district court has the ministerio público requested reparation of damage. He generally cites the economic incapacity of the defendant in excusing the defendant from the responsibility of restitution. The reparation of damage clause, with available penal personnel, is also nonenforceable.

A CASE OF NO CONTEST

The following case of homicide, which traveled through the Oaxaca state system of appeals, is not representative of cases appealed from the villages of the Villa Alta district. It merely represents relationships and roles in the official system.

On April 10, 1964, Cipriano, a truck driver in the transport cooperative Sierra Alta, based in Oaxaca City, was in the city to load his truck with cargo to take the next day into the southern region of the district of Villa Alta. He went alone that evening to a small cantina, La Morenita, which was near the cooperative warehouse, a few blocks from Oaxaca's central square. Around eleven, after Cipriano had drunk a few beers, Ernesto, a recently hired driver in the cooperative, and Chico, Ernesto's helper and work companion on his trips along the dirt roads of the Sierras, walked into La Morenita and ordered beers. Ernesto and Chico were already drunk.

As the men conversed, Ernesto and Chico began to throw out indirect insults at Cipriano concerning his capabilities as a trucker compared with their own. Cipriano said that because of his seniority as a trucker and as a worker in the cooperative he was their father on the road. Neither Ernesto nor Chico countenanced Cipriano's claim of paternity, and they headed toward him. Cipriano tried to defend himself, but the two managed to kick him and punch him in the face before the owner of the cantina intervened and separated them. Cipriano, at the owner's command, went to another room in the cantina. The owner detained Ernesto and Chico and tried to calm them down. Ernesto and Chico then left the cantina but waited outside for Cipriano. The owner, noticing that the two men were outside, took Cipriano home.

This fight was the beginning of a violent dispute. For nearly a month, whenever the opponents ran into each other in the cooperative office and in Sierra villages, they did not speak, except once, when Cipriano told Ernesto, "There in Ralu'a we met and there we will leave it."

On Monday, April 26, a market day, all three men happened to be in Ralu'a. After a day of heavy drinking, Cipriano ended up in late afternoon in the cantina of Urbano Vargas Mejia, at Ralu'a's marketplace. As he sat at a table drinking beer, sometime between 5:00 and 5:30, Ernesto and Chico entered the cantina, walked up to the counter, and started drinking. As the two companions were on their second beer, Cipriano walked over to them and the three began to quarrel. Urbano, the owner of the cantina, was at the opposite end of the counter. Noticing the quarrel and fearing a fight, Urbano sent his wife to summon the municipal police.

Suddenly Cipriano, in the midst of the quarrel, extended his hand to Ernesto and said, "Why don't we be friends?" Just as Cipriano held out his hand, Chico punched him. Then Ernesto pushed Cipriano and began to kick him. Cipriano reached under his belt for an unsheathed knife he used for cutting rope and canvas. He drew the knife and stabbed Chico in the stomach. Ernesto tried to push Cipriano aside and flee. Cipriano jabbed at Ernesto and stabbed him in the side under his arm.

Ernesto ran out of the cantina. He saw Cipriano run out, too, headed toward Ralu'a's municipal building with the knife in his hand. Ernesto went back inside and found Chico slumped in a chair holding his stomach.

When Urbano realized that Chico had been seriously injured, he sent for a medical student interning in Ralu'a. As the student was treating Chico, a member of the municipal police force arrived, then left to notify Ralu'a's síndico and other municipal authorities of the stabbing. Urbano's wife had been unable to locate the municipal police for several minutes because they were walking through Ralu'a collecting taxes from residents and vendors in the marketplace.

At the municipal building, Cipriano laid his knife on a table in front of the municipal authorities, who were holding court. He told them what had happened and urged them to go to the cantina. They did not jail him, but the síndico and the *regidores,* the directors of the local police force, left for Urbano's cantina to verify the story. At the cantina they decided that both wounded men should be taken to the municipal building for continued treatment by the medical student. Chico was covered with a sheet and carried on a wooden plank.

Back at the municipal building, the authorities placed Cipriano in jail. That evening Cipriano, Ernesto, and Urbano testified before Ralu'a's alcalde. As the alcalde took the testimony, the secretary of Ralu'a's municipal government and court recorded it. The medical student also recorded a description of Ernesto's stab wounds.

After testifying, Ernesto was taken to another location for continued treatment. Around 3:30 Tuesday morning the authorities notified him that Chico had died as a result of the stab wound.

Later in the day the alcalde, with friends of Chico present, formally identified the body. Also that day, before Chico was lowered into his grave, the medical student performed an autopsy and recorded a description of Chico's wound. The alcalde prepared the death certificate and closed the official municipal court investigation. Village police then walked Cipriano the eight hours to Villa Alta. They handed their prisoner over to the ministerio público, along with the recorded investigation. Ralu'a's alcalde accused Cipriano of bodily injury and homicide.

On receipt of the documents and the prisoner the ministerio público placed Cipriano in the district jail, then initiated his own investigation of the charges. By letter, he notified the procurador general in Oaxaca City of his initiation of the case. With both Ernesto and Cipriano present the ministerio público on April 30 asked the two parties if they ratified the declaration they offered to the alcalde of Ralu'a. Then he asked additional questions concerning the circumstances surrounding the acts of April 26. The ministerio público then sent his write-up of the testimony, along with that of the Ralu'a investigation, next door to the office of the district judge. The ministerio público also charged Cipriano with bodily injury and homicide.

On May 2, the district judge formally initiated an investigation of the charges. He sent a letter to the president of the State Superior Court notifying him of case initiation. The judge called Cipriano to the door of the court, which opens onto the courtyard of the district jail, and took down the prisoner's account of what happened on April 26. He also asked questions concerning the acts. Then he prepared the act of formal imprisonment of Cipriano.

On May 4, the judge asked Urbano, who was in Villa Alta at the judge's demand, if he ratified his previous testimony. After Urbano answered in the affirmative the judge questioned him further. The next day Ernesto ratified and amplified his declaration. The same day the judge brought Cipriano to the jail door and, with Ernesto present, notified the two men of contradictions in their testimony. He then initiated the careo, in which the accused and witnesses against him discuss their disagreements. Cipriano and Ernesto did not enter into discussion, however, and merely stated that they upheld their previous declarations. The careo between Cipriano and Urbano was also unproductive.

On May 28, with Cipriano still held prisoner in Villa Alta, the district judge ordered the court secretary to search into the past ten years of court records to determine if Cipriano had any penal antecedents. A member of the Villa Alta police force, appointed as keeper of the jail, testified in the judge's office that Cipriano had maintained good conduct while in jail. The judge also recorded statements by two prisoners who testified to the good behavior of Cipriano. The judge introduced into the case record a letter from the medical student in Ralu'a listing, on the basis of his own examination, the estimated time that Ernesto's wound would take to heal and whether the wound would in any way be incapacitating.

When the district judge received the medical student's autopsy report in the original Ralu'a investigation, he sent the report to paramedics, or *perito prácticos* in medicine, assigned to the State Superior Court in Oaxaca City. On May 28, the judge entered into case records a letter from the perito prácticos citing, definitively for the case, hemorrhaging in the abdominal cavity resulting from a stab wound as the cause of Chico's death.

The next step in Cipriano's case came almost three months later when on August 20 the district judge ordered Cipriano to be taken to the state penitentiary in Oaxaca City, a move that Cipriano had requested. State judicial police traveled from Oaxaca City to Villa Alta and escorted Cipriano to the penitentiary.

On September 10, the district judge formally closed the district investigation into the charges against Cipriano. On October 14, he sent the case to the ministerio público and asked him to formulate his conclusions within five days. The ministerio público recommended sentences found in the state penal code for bodily injury and homicide. Before submitting his recommendations for sentencing to the district judge, the ministerio público mailed them to the procurador general in Oaxaca City for his comments. He modified the ministerio público's conclusions, calling for the sentences required for bodily injury and homicide committed in self-defense.

On January 19, 1965, the *juez tercero,* or third penal judge, in Oaxaca City notified Cipriano, in the state penitentiary, of the sentence that had been reached by the ministerio público and modified by the procurador general. Cipriano's assigned defense lawyer was also notified of the conclusions. Neither notified the third judge or the Villa Alta district judge of their agreement or disagreement with the prosecutor's recommendations for sentencing.

On February 2, the district judge formulated his conclusions in the sentencing of Cipriano. Through the third judge, he notified Cipriano and his defender as well as the ministerio público that he would formally pronounce sentence in Villa Alta on February 7. That meant that he would type up his conclusions at his desk in the Villa Alta district court.

In his sentence, pronounced nine months and one week after the commission of the crimes, the district judge found sufficient proof to determine that both crimes had been committed and that the accused, Cipriano, was their perpetrator. He modified the charges to bodily injury and homicide committed in self-defense, however, and sentenced Cipriano accordingly. For a crime of bodily injury that does not put the victim's life in jeopardy the Oaxaca state penal code recommends three days to four months in prison and a fine of fifty pesos. The code also states that if the accused is found guilty of more than one crime, the sentence shall correspond to the crime that merits the greater penalty—in this case, homicide committed in self-defense—and that sentence may be augmented for a period equal to half its maximum length. For homicide in self-defense the state penal code recommends four to twelve years in prison.

On February 7, the district judge imposed the sentence of twelve years in prison, counting as its date of commencement the day Cipriano was imprisoned in Ralu'a. The judge also absolved Cipriano's wife of paying damages to the injured parties. The governor of the state was to determine where Cipriano would serve his term. The third judge in Oaxaca City notified both Cipriano and his defender on May 12 of the sentence. Cipriano notified the third judge that he wished to appeal.

On November 21, the seven magistrates of the State Superior Court formulated their conclusions in Cipriano's appeal. They concurred with the district judge in his finding of guilt but did not uphold the judge's sentence, reducing it from twelve to five years in prison.

Two years later, on October 4, 1967, the district judge received a letter from an aide to the subsecretary of the secretary general of the cabinet of the state of Oaxaca asking him to supply information concerning wrongs committed by Cipriano while in prison, the conduct he had maintained in prison, any exterior manifestations he may have shown of repentance or correction, any inclinations he demonstrated while in prison, and cases in process against him. The chief of the Villa Alta police submitted a statement providing this information. It contained no negative criticisms of Cipriano's behavior.

On December 26, 1967, the governor of Oaxaca signed Cipriano's *salvo conducta*, his formal release from prison. The release said that Cipriano had to agree not to leave his stated address in Oaxaca City without permission. If he did, the attorney general would be notified and would proceed against him accordingly. It also said that Cipriano had to present himself before the chief of the state police on the twenty-sixth of every month for twenty months. The secretary general of Oaxaca's cabinet, who was also chief of the Department of Governance, sent a copy of the salvo conducta to the head of Oaxaca state police and to the third judge in Oaxaca City. The head of the Oaxaca state penitentiary presented the salvo conducta to Cipriano, and he was released.

NOTES TO THE CHAPTERS

CHAPTER 1 INTRODUCTION: A MARKETPLACE REGION

1. Internal centralization is taking place through the proliferation of local leadership roles among village residents and those who have migrated to cities but actively participate in village politics and economy. External centralization is developing through two channels. Some village groups now follow policy formulated by authorities of centralized hierarchical religious organizations new to village life. These newly arrived religions are represented by both village and regional assemblies. The second channel is regional political assemblies which, though lacking a clear hierarchical structure, find organizational leadership within two villages. Some villages, village groups, and factions use the assemblies (that is, each other) to formulate approaches and responses to village conflicts and conflicts with external institutions. These forms of centralization have developed through the choices of villagers to coalesce and align.

2. The *agencia* is supposed to report offenses to public order and infractions of state law to its *municipio* (see appendix, p. ooo). Agencias in the Villa Alta marketplace region, such as Taguí, which is an agencia of Villa Alta, generally handle problems within the village rather than seeking the help of their municipios. Municipios most often do not attempt to assert authority over agencias or actively seek out their disputes for municipal courts. Although the populations of agencias are often included in the population figures of municipios, in the Villa Alta marketplace region, the two act as independent and separate sociopolitical systems. The alliances they develop are not based on the municipio-agencia relationship.

3. My translation.

4. This figure is based on a household composition census I conducted in Villa Alta in 1984. Urban Villaltecos, students, and employees who own homes in Villa Alta but work elsewhere are not included in these figures. There is now frequent visiting between Oaxaca City, Mexico City, and Villa Alta. The population of the district seat swells during the summer months when Villalteco students and schoolteachers return to their homes or families. Urban Villaltecos also return for fiestas and family events. Urban Villaltecos are members of the village community and play important economic, political and legal roles within it, though they are not included in the population figures. I also do not include residents of Villa Alta's agencias, which are included in official population figures for the municipio.

5. Chance (1978b) and de la Fuente (1949) published selections of dockets

from these archives, which were moved to Oaxaca City in 1984. Parnell (1978a) analyzed dockets of 1920–74.

6. The *municipio libre* is a semiautonomous political unit that elects its own government. The municipios in the Villa Alta district, including the district seat, act politically and legally as closed corporate communities (Wolf 1955). Integrated by law into state administrative and legal systems, elected village governments and legal officials nonetheless reserve the right to act independently of centralized policy. They enforce local custom. An effective strategy used by village presidents when asked to cooperate with a district investigation into village disputes is to claim prior local administrative commitments that do not allow time for legal investigations. For further information about the municipio libre in Oaxaca see Perez Jimenez (1955).

7. Conflicts and disputes are most often distinguished by placing them along a public-private continuum. As conflicts move into public arenas or expand to include a third party, they become disputes. Most conflicts to which I refer in Villa Alta are political or familial disagreements and rivalries that have historical components and have endured over time into the present. These conflicts are often unvoiced components of disputes that develop across factional, party, or familial lines. Some disputes develop as symbolic expressions of such conflicts. Other disputes transform as they develop into open expressions of political or familial conflicts, the original conflict between parties long forgotten or blurred by smoldering animosities.

8. Kearney (1972, p. 41) attributes similar fear of internal conflicts and a desire for "internal unity and solidarity" among the Zapotec villagers of Ixtepeji in the district of Ixtlán.

9. For further discussion of the structure and dynamics of dendritic market systems see C. Smith (1976b) and Johnson (1970).

10. The activities of the Comisión del Compra de Café, though oriented toward increased coffee cultivation in marketplace villages, have focused on the technology of cultivation of fields already dedicated to the cash crop. In Villa Alta, where coffee growers are most receptive to the aid of the commission, increased fertilization of coffee fields is the major result of the commission's work. There is little increase in the use of irrigation and nurseries (*viveros*), more common practices in villages of the Talea region. I do not have figures for the amount of land allocated for increased coffee production in the marketplace region since the arrival of the commission, but accounts of villagers and members of the commission indicate there has been little change. Villaltecos, for example, are seeking alternatives to coffee, the most common choice being *pimienta* (black pepper), perhaps in response to fluctuations in coffee prices and a scarcity of labor for implementing more extensive coffee production and technological changes. Because coffee plants mature and become productive after five to seven years, the dedication of more time and land to coffee cultivation can bring havoc to personal economies in subsistence-level villages during the maturation period when subsistence crop production has decreased yet a cash surplus is only a promise of the future. It does not appear that this is the reason for lesser Zapotec participation in the Villa Alta marketplace.

11. Hirabayashi (1983) mentions two prior regional associations that formed within the district, one in 1960 and the other in the early 1970s. Both were short-lived and, it appears, included representatives of villages rather than village factions and groups.

12. Mexico's economic crisis was worsened by the optimism that preceded it during the years 1977–82, fueled by petroleum discoveries and buttressed by economic borrowing. Falling international prices for oil and overborrowing led to devaluations of the peso, default on foreign debts, sharp reductions in purchasing power, and inflation that reached almost one hundred percent in 1982 and an estimated sixty percent in 1984. In addition, no resolution of the crisis appeared possible in the near future. The crisis was heightened by charges of corruption against former President Lopez Portillo and his associates, who allegedly expropriated enormous sums from oil revenues and external borrowing for personal use (Sanders 1986). Faith in the ability of government leaders to put the economy of Mexico in order lessened, and challenges from opposition parties mounted. The crisis was accompanied by multiplying reports of political oppression and by revolution in Mexico's neighbors El Salvador, Guatemala, and Nicaragua, which sent waves of refugees into southern Mexico and Mexican cities.

13. No *haciendas* were located in the Villa Alta district (Nader 1969b, p. 335). As a result, the disassembling of haciendas following the Revolution did not lead to the extensive formation of *ejidos* (communal lands) in Villa Alta (Beals 1975, p. 220).

14. Parnell (1978a, 1978b) provides analysis of district court cases and case patterns as they vary from state and national procedural and criminal codes.

15. A person or topic is "dancing in the mouths of the people" when the subject of local gossip.

CHAPTER 2 THE CASE OF THE PADRE'S KEYS

1. During February and March, farmers burn brush and trees on the plots where they will plant corn in April, after the rainy season begins. Also in April the new white blooms appear in the recently harvested coffee fields.

2. Land for the technical school, like that for roads, was appropriated from individual owners by the federal government. The land on which the technical school stands was owned by Tito Mendiolea, civil recorder for the district court.

3. Calero and the elder Negrete are half-brothers. Their families live together in a compound near the central square.

4. The mayordoma in Villa Alta is custodian of public spaces within the Catholic church during the day and sells candles in the church. Though her responsibilities do not include the organization or presentation of church ceremonies or events, the mayordoma holds the highest formal position of responsibility among females in the district seat.

5. Reports of the seminarian's attitude toward money were subsequently spread by Blasco to argue that he was irresponsible and by friends of the seminarian to argue that he was not a thief.

6. Espinosa's legal wife and his mother, who lived in his house, were not active participants in this network. Espinosa also had a common-law wife and children in another part of the village. This widely discussed relationship may have affected his wife's social activities in Villa Alta.

7. Like Luisa, most other women in Villa Alta with children by bureaucrats who abandoned them do not marry but follow a pattern of serial monogamy.

8. The judge can contest a prosecutor's decision not to request the filing of charges against an accused party.

9. The church committee prepares and coordinates all secular and religious fiesta events. The kitchen committee prepares meals for visiting bands and serves them.

10. In this talk, Espinosa compared his political position to that of a telegraph line troubleshooter who must pull from two directions at one time to repair a broken line.

11. This image of Christ was made in Guatemala.

12. The alliance between Villa Alta and Zacatepec is an old one. Luis Rodriguez, formerly the most powerful cacique in the Mixe district and native of Zacatepec, was married to a Villalteca. The Villalteco mero cacique David Mendiolea has commercial ties to Zacatepec.

13. During the calenda, ties of friendship are renewed among residents and those from Oaxaca City and Mexico City who are attending the fiesta.

14. The Caleros knew that Espinosa would learn about the plan through an ally—the cantina owner who was present during the discussion.

15. Villagers customarily pay their fees before the fiesta begins. For this fiesta more than three-fourths of the household heads paid during the fiesta or after it was over.

16. Some voiced the opinion that this had been the Calero plan all along.

17. Women also participate in formal village meetings in the district villages of Juquila Vijanos and Yalálag.

18. Court officials augment their incomes by demanding fees to process the papers for government loans to farmers. However, most are paid to stockfarmers and to my knowledge stock-farming is not an important specialization in any of the district villages. Court officials therefore describe Villa Alta as the least desirable post in the state.

CHAPTER 3 DIVISION IN THE DISTRICT SEAT

1. Although service in cargo system positions is termed voluntary (unpaid), it is considered a duty for village males. In Villa Alta, however, the demands of work are an acceptable excuse for avoiding service in cargos for employees, especially those who teach in other villages, but not for campesinos.

2. The village secretary (*secretario*) is now a salaried position and not in practice part of the cargo system.

3. In 1984, the coffee of two Villalteco Progressives remained unpicked in the absence of Zapotec laborers willing to work in their fields.

4. Mendiolea owned the only two buses that traveled between Villa Alta and Oaxaca City on the older road. With the opening of the Calero-sponsored road, which was safer and more dependable, a Oaxaca City transport company ran one bus daily between Villa Alta and the state capital. The first road is maintained by villages along it. The federal government maintains the new road. Most villagers choose the new road, and that has brought financial hardship to the Mendiolea line.

5. *Amparo,* which was established in articles 103 and 107 of the Mexican Constitution of 1917, is similar to writs of habeas corpus, mandamus, error, and injunction (Baker 1971). My interviews with villagers of the region suggested that few were aware of their rights to judicial review or how to demand it. Baker provides a comprehensive study of the amparo suit to Mexico.

6. Side effects of the policy of decentralization were 1) increased local economic dependence on government funds; 2) increased animosity between the seat and other district villagers who opposed it as the site of the district administrative center; and 3) a decrease in the local supply of labor for coffee growers.

7. Gil's completion of a new municipal building, which also contained new telegraph and postal offices, was accomplished primarily through a federal assistance policy formulated without Gil's participation. Both Gil and Blasco depended on Mendiolea for brokerage ties to politicians and developmental agencies.

8. The major stigma of PRI in Villa Alta was its use of force, reportedly deadly at times, to deal with journalists and vocal leaders of opposition groups such as labor unions.

9. Villaltecos who worried about Zapotec opposition were concerned about the decreasing number of vendors of agricultural produce in the Monday marketplace. They also feared that the regional assemblies hoped to relocate the district seat to San Francisco Cajonos in the region of Yalálag, a headquarters for the assemblies. San Francisco Cajonos was connected to similar groups on the Oaxacan coast.

10. Continued inflation and national economic crises gave force to Calero arguments against villager participation in Progressive projects through the donation of time and money. Prices and economic problems were, along with disputes, the most common topics of daily conversation.

11. Prior to this change, an older minifundista who was considered socially marginal had been mayordomo. He had not held a position in the civil cargo system.

12. Intergenerational conflicts between Villalteco leaders organized and heated political conflicts, while relations of kinship, cooperation, compadrazgo, and friendship among their followers provided ties of communication across political groups. These ties were the social channels through which disputes could spread, but the reciprocity they carried inhibited the escalation of disputes.

13. Villaltecos, like the Zapotec, refer to respected elders of ascending generations as aunt (*tía*) and uncle (*tío*). Although Esperanza Blasco was a

distant cousin of the Zarcos, they called her tía. Blasco chose to honor her kinship ties to many of the Zarco women through mutual aid and sharing of surplus.

14. Pluralization of the seat occurred through increased economic stratification (greater differences in the earnings of latifundistas and minifundistas), occupational specialization (professionalization of native Villaltecos and growth in the number of specialized day laborers), and ethnic diversification (growth in the number of Zapotec, Chinantec, and Mixe residents).

CHAPTER 4 THE ANATOMY OF A DISPUTE

1. When a bureaucrat violated state or federal law through a nonviolent offense, district and village court officials notified the offender's administrative director rather than initiating a legal case. They also followed this procedure in response to some violent offenses.

2. Villagers on both sides recognized involvement of the ministerio público in the dispute as a show of weakness by the padre and inappropriate to the personal relationship between the padre and the seminarian. This move raised the stakes for those who supported the padre.

3. The ministerio público could not establish through formal testimony that the padre owned the items he claimed were stolen.

4. The court has detained witnesses in the district jail without filing charges, then fined the detainees for their release. Also, offering false testimony in court may become a permanent stigma. Such a stigma limits one's access to information and authority in the development of disputes. For women, it may also lead to exclusion from important social activities.

5. According to Villaltecos, it was the first nonviolent organized political protest by the Zapotec in the district seat. In addition to demonstrating newly found Zapotec alliances and economic power, the visit made it clear that the district was becoming smaller through federal development and maintenance of new roads that extended not only to Oaxaca City but also to Totontepec and Camotlán. The road was to continue on to Choapan.

6. Though Calero and Progressive leaders represented types of village relationships to external institutions rather than the exact policies of these institutions, their local political identities attached these institutions to village political and intergenerational conflicts.

7. In 1984, Progressives, headed by Espinosa, mounted a successful effort to remove a native Villalteco teacher from his position in the seat's state-funded secondary school (not the federal ETA) because he had refused on religious grounds to serve on village committees and in the cargo system and did not pay the resulting fines or wages for a replacement.

8. Through their social ties the women moved information from the small, intimate networks of their male kin into the public voice. Men used the female networks to develop dispute-based political negotiations.

9. Through baptismal records kept in the village church, the padre held the

key to important descent information. In Villa Alta, monogamy exists in public statements to a much greater degree than in practice.

10. Most non-Villalteco students and ETA faculty members roomed and purchased meals in Lachirioag.

CHAPTER 5 VILLAGE DIVISIONS AND REGIONAL ALLIANCES

1. The village Witnesses did not allow music or dancing. Formerly, the Taguí band played at fiestas in the marketplace region and in the eastern lowlands of the district of Choapan. For further discussion of alliances nurtured through fiesta-based exchanges see W. Smith (1977).

2. Witnesses collectively worked land separate from village land, which was divided into individually cultivated plots.

3. State law allows village courts to incarcerate citizens for no more than three days.

4. This case prompted a special meeting of Lachirioag citizens at the ruins of the first Catholic church in the marketplace region located in Analco, a barrio of Villa Alta. This meeting reaffirmed Lachirioag as a Catholic village, lessening schisms widened in the disputes of 1983. Lachirioaltecos did not refer this case to the ministerio público. Village officials cannot legally take human life as punishment for a wrong, although villages do at times eliminate recidivists in this way. The ministerio público and district judge were aware of the hanging in Lachirioag but chose not to intervene.

5. Village courts demand restitution in cases of theft, property damage, and injury. If a party found guilty does not replace, repair, or return stolen or damaged property, property of equal value belonging to the offender is confiscated by the village government and given to the victim.

6. The Department of Governance manages Mexico's internal political problems, including those related to elections and the legal jurisdictions of political units, such as relations between municipios and agencias.

7. Most villages in the district claim political alignment with PRI (Institutional Revolutionary Party), which was established in 1929 as the National Revolutionary Party and has controlled the presidency and all governorships since then. PRI is often characterized as centrist to left along the political spectrum. Most who have opposed PRI by supporting other parties have aligned with PAN (National Action Party), which was founded in 1939, is strongest in northern border states, and voices policies generally to the right of PRI, calling for less government participation in the national economy. There are several other political parties in Mexico, but the new party that has gained the most supporters in the Villa Alta district over the past decade is the United Mexican Socialist Party (PSUM), which was founded in 1978 and is generally thought to support policies to the left of PRI.

8. The weakness of PRI's influence over local views is also noted by Kearney (1972, p. 42) for the Zapotec village of Ixtepeji in the district of Ixtlán where "the politics and ideology of PRI are irrelevant. . . . What is important is to be

solidly united with the government and not allow anything to disrupt this unity, that is, to ensure that the entire town presents 'a single front.' "

9. For a discussion of differences between ideal norms and pragmatic norms, or the interpretation of principles through practical considerations, see Bailey (1969).

CHAPTER 6 STATE LAW OR VILLAGE LAW

1. The primary purpose of my initial research in Villa Alta was to study village social organization and villager use of the Oaxaca state legal system of appeals. Although I conducted much of my research on village society in the district seat, I expanded it into the larger region to gather data for controlled comparison of village patterns of appeals. Since the Zapotec villages share so many economic, political, and cultural characteristics, comparing differences in the social organizations of villages against this background of similarities elucidated the influence of society on legal choices and development. The same type of comparison was possible between Zapotec villages and the district seat since they are economically and culturally different but have similar civil-religious organizations. Excellent examples of analysis based on controlled comparisons and regional research are Geertz (1963) and C. Smith (1976a).

2. Colson (1974, p. 78) cites similar dynamics in relations between "egalitarian peoples" in Africa and newly instituted colonial courts. She writes that this relationship "rests upon the dichotomy of experience between those who live within the community and can be assumed to know its ways and those who occupy the upper echelons of power who are neither drawn from the community nor live within it. Inevitably, the latter are sealed off from local knowledge vital to the running of ordinary activities, and the information they receive is carefully controlled.

3. For further discussion of Oaxacan district courts and their dockets see Hunt and Hunt (1969). Parnell (1978a and 1978b) provides examples of procedural patterns in cases processed by the district court. Cases ended most frequently as the result of the discontinuation of the flow of information from a village to the district court. Court officials often could not process cases because of the absence of witnesses or an accused. Also, new district court judges or secretaries often did not resume case investigations initiated by their predecessors.

4. The Villa Alta district court recorder compiled the population statistics. The number of cases appealed is based on my own count from reading case records rather than on district court dockets. My count increases the number of appealed cases beyond the official record. Some *procesos* (case records) contain complaints for offenses that occurred at different times (occasionally over a period of several years). Though some procesos are, therefore, records of court use within extended cases of disputing, they may represent several decisions to appeal at different times within an ongoing dispute.

5. Aligned political bosses, often from the same extended family, cooperate

in the control of village affairs. Nonaligned bosses are opponents and offer villagers alternative policies. Aligned political bosses are similar to village *principales,* or elders who have successfully passed through the cargo system and have formed an informal council that establishes policy for elected village officials. Political bosses, however, achieve their power not through age or through the fulfillment of cargos but more often through wealth and command of the Spanish language.

6. The tendency to appeal cases to the district court does not mean that villagers approve of appeal or that they will cooperate with a district court investigation initiated by appeal. However, the same village organizational fissures through which cases travel to Villa Alta may also weaken attempts by villagers to resist district court investigations.

7. Discussion of the functions of law assume that law is a symbolic system used by persons and groups to achieve their own ends. Laws may also express the ideals of those who control them. Individuals use law to govern, but law does not govern the thoughts of individuals. Nader and Todd (1978, pp. 1–40), Comaroff and Roberts (1977), Gulliver (1979), Gluckman (1963), Kuper and Kuper (1965), Unger (1976), Coser (1956), and Colson (1953) discuss the functions of law in various types of social systems.

8. Llewellyn and Hoebel (1941), Colson (1953), Barton (1919), and other researchers used cases of disputing to examine law as it existed in daily relationships—outside the formal or official legal contexts that were the focus of Western legal studies and analysis. Missing from their analyses was a definition of law and legal terminology researchers could apply universally without extreme distortion of social and cultural differences. Studies of law adopted the dispute as a concept and the dispute case study as a methodology to generate data for comparison across cultures and types of legal forums. Dispute settlement and legal processes became a focus of legal studies. Several researchers have worked to refine the study of dispute as a unit of social analysis, including Van Velsen (1967), Epstein (1967), Gluckman (1973), and Parnell (1982).

9. In Villa Alta, ongoing expanded disputes generate disagreements as individuals (dyads) who join in the disputing argue and negotiate over various developing rationales. Individuals may attach their disagreements to ongoing disputes in the public arena. Ongoing disputes have a magnetic effect on disagreements, attracting them into the realm of public disputing.

10. A major concern of disputants in Villa Alta is the effect a dispute may have on social relationships. The principles villagers apply in dispute management and the choice of dispute forums are based on their analysis of their own social systems and are sociological in nature, as Selby (1974) found in a Zapotec village in the Valley of Oaxaca.

Bernal (1958, p. 6) called the Valley Zapotec an "introvert culture, which tends not to accept change from the outside and is quite content to go along its own way. . . . There seems to be always an inner development having very little or no connection with the outside." My study reveals similar qualities among the Sierra Zapotec. Their assertion of the ethic of local control and development may, however, be a cultural "trait" institutionalized by colonization through the municipio libre. Placing the local political unit as a priority above all others requires a means of expression once economic exchange unites local and urban systems. The village social system provides the means through its civil-religious organization. The fact that Villaltecos are not Zapotec indicates that introversion may be a product of society. For more on the Zapotec world view see Leslie (1960), Nader (1966), and Parsons (1936).

Gluckman (1955, 1965, 1969), Malinowski (1926, 1961), Pospisil (1968), Smith and Roberts (1954), and Spradley (1970) examine relationships between group-based values and law. Glacken (1967) offers an interesting discussion of relationships between ideas, social philosophies, and the expansion of social systems.

11. For example, when women of Villa Alta enter into disputes with women from Lachirioag (who are reputed to have healing powers), they accuse their neighbors of witchcraft while claiming that women of Villa Alta do not use witchcraft. Lachirioaltecas cannot then be integrated into Villalteco society solely through legal processes but must undergo a change of identity through migration or marriage.

12. The Talean court combines mediation with adjudication. The village presidente may attempt both to persuade and to coerce disputants to reach an agreement through drawing on knowledge of both disputant relationships and village consensus. Nader (1969a) describes the outcome of most Talean court cases as "compromise arrived at by adjudication or, in some cases, adjudication based on compromise."

13. In the process of dispute expansion, the way disputants value or prioritize their associations with various levels differs over time. Though a disputant may be first of all a member of a family, then as the dispute expands a member of a political group, a regional assembly, or an urban network, the membership that achieves priority in the end is the village. Ethnographers have studied levels as cognitive categories through which groups organize their social relations, some concluding (Adams 1975) that cross-cultural evidence shows that the number of such levels humans can utilize is limited. Discussions of levels of relations from a comparative perspective and in specific cultural contexts may be found in Bailey (1960), Bohannon (1965), Pospisil (1967, 1968, 1971), Ravicz (1965), Starr (1954), Steward (1955), and Wolf (1967).

14. Colson (1974) points out many of the benefits of the use of local codes in situations of conflict between local custom and the written laws of a centralized system. Unwritten tradition is more flexible and changeable than codified law. The use of local knowledge to explore disputes and problems restricts participation in them to those who are directly affected by their outcomes. Avoidance of state courts prevents the codification of custom or tradition which would limit its usefulness as a flexible language through which villagers can innovate in response to changing conditions. Colson (1974, p. 81) writes, "A code in the hands of a foreign administrator who assumes that it means what it says becomes an instrument of repression and a foe to the imaginative innovation which can go on only so long as the local people are the sole repositories of the legitimizing tradition. Their innovation has to stand the test of popular approval, or at least the mobilization of strong support, but that

is determined by the effectiveness of the innovation in dealing with the current situation, rather than by its faithfulness to a dimly remembered and not necessarily honored past.

CHAPTER 7 DISPUTING AND CENTRALIZATION

1. Pluralism—the organization of ethnic and economic differences in village society—is a social and symbolic resource that gives conceptual order to the diversity perceived in the external world. Various studies examine the effect of pluralism on social relations and societal development, though without a general theory, including Barth (1969), Benedict (1962), Jackson (1977), Kuper and Smith (1969), and Shibutani and Kwan (1965).

2. Persons in multiplex relationships are interdependent, have ties of reciprocity related to more than one common purpose and identity, and play more than one important social role for each other. For example, a Villalteco may work on committees with a neighbor who may also be a kinsman and compadre who worships at the same church. In contrast, a Villalteco is more likely to have a simplex relationship with a villager from Taguí—one based solely on exchanging goods in the marketplace. The loss of a multiplex relationship is more punitive than the loss of a simplex relationship. Disputants in multiplex relationships tend to seek ways to mend their ties.

3. *Capitalism* and *state* refer to concepts as well as to specific forms of enterprise, institutions, and relationships. Some of the literature on culture contact treats these two terms as forces, such as surplus-producing or centralizing forces, that are uniform and consistent. My cases show that Sierra villagers personalize external institutions and forces and develop their own ideas about them. They experience these influences as neither uniform nor consistent but varying, unpredictable, and personal—actually as human forces with human characteristics.

4. As facilitators of exchange between two or more parties that do not or cannot develop such relationships for themselves, brokers are entrepreneurs who depend on the maintenance of social, geographic, or cultural distance between the groups they link. To sustain their brokerage roles and increase their power they must maintain that distance as well as the interdependence of their clients. For further discussion of the roles of brokers, gatekeepers, and intermediaries see Anderson (1969), Barnes (1968), Boissevain (1974), Geertz (1965), Mayer (1961), Silverman (1965), and Witty (1981).

5. Turner (1957) described segmentary oppositions as they exist in acephalous segmentary states of Africa. Evans-Pritchard (1940) stated that Nuer tribes were split into segments. He described the structural principle of segmentation and the opposition between segments (p. 142): "Each segment is itself segmented and there is opposition between its parts. The members of any segment unite against adjacent segments of the same order and unite with these segments against larger sections." Individuals see themselves as members of the smaller segments to which they belong and of larger, more inclusive segments only when they join with them to oppose a common foe. Segments

fuse and individuals show allegiance to their tribe only when fighting a common enemy.

6. In Villa Alta, a compromise defines the village's relationship to an external factor but also states the relative power of the Caleros and the Progressives. For example, the Progressives, who limit the local political role of the Catholic church, gained support in the 1984 disputes. In this way, the relative power of the two political groups and the village's relationship to external institutions vary over time in response to external factors. Leach (1954) described a similar system that operated in Kachin settlements of highland Burma. Two distinctively different socioeconomic systems coexisted within the same societies. Each system achieved dominance at different times. The political behavior of the Kachin was a compromise between the polarized political doctrines. Graburn (1969) described the changing dominance of two systems of law in Eskimo settlements in response to changing ecological conditions.

7. Gibbs (1963) described the therapeutic qualities of moots among the Kpelle in central Liberia, where disputants negotiated and mediated in settings open to interested parties. The moot was relatively free of normative restrictions and rules of evidence; it led to catharsis and the removal of bitterness among disputants through the venting of spleens, reunited disputants in ongoing peaceful relationships through the manipulation of highly valued symbols, and was educational.

8. Paul Bohannon (1980, p. 520) claimed that peasant communities were disappearing into a "multispecial-purpose-communities-cum-network social structure" characteristic of the United States. He was referring to Hine's article (1977) in which she referred to an emerging form of alliance among the powerless organizing for social structural change as a "segmented polycephalous network" (SPIN). A SPIN is decentralized and polycentric, "composed of autonomous segments which are organizationally self-sufficient, any of which could survive the elimination of the others" (p. 19). The segments are integrated by horizontal organizational linkages and a shared conceptual framework—a few basic assumptions. Within a SPIN, a tendency toward fission-fusion characterizes relations among its segments. Hine (p. 22) stated that there was "increasing evidence of many middle-range regional and transnational networks cutting across traditional vertical lines of power."

Regional political assemblies in Villa Alta appear to conform to Hine's model of the SPIN, with common regional oppositions as a unifying force. A hierarchical structure may be emerging, however, as two district villages, Camotlán and San Francisco Cajonos are becoming meeting places and nodes of communication to allied SPINS in Oaxaca City and along the Oaxacan coast.

9. What constitutes change in a society is a matter of frequent discussion among social scientists. Sierra village law is changing primarily through the elaboration, expansion, and centralization of the relationships and conceptual frameworks in which villagers enact local disputes. Yet these changes are the product both of contact with forces outside the village and, by villager choice, of the extension of legal processes traditional to village life into broader social contexts. Various studies discuss the forces and nature of social and legal change, including Allot (1961), Anderson (1963), Barkun (1971), Barth

(1967), Bendix (1967), Cancian (1972), Cohn (1959), Collier (1973), Fallers (1969), Felstiner (1974), Firth (1954), Foster (1967), Goody (1975), I.F.E. University (1971), Taylor (1979), Kuper and Kuper (1965), Moore (1970), and Redfield (1962).

10. Colson (1974, p. 62) reaches a conclusion that appears to be applicable here: "Lewis Henry Morgan's belief that societies change because men seek to better their lot and to find solutions to the evils of their condition may be less foolish than it appeared to be in the days when we believed with Durkheim that men sacralized their societies and revered the conditions in which they found themselves."

GLOSSARY OF SPANISH TERMS

agencia: political residential unit of fewer than 2000 inhabitants

agente municipal: elected head of the agencia

agente de policía: elected head of residential unit of fewer than 200 inhabitants

agentes de ministerio público auxiliares, adscritos, and investigadores: officials appointed by the procurador as the representatives in district penal affairs

aguardiente: hard liquor distilled from sugarcane

alcalde: judge, mayor

amparo: similar to writs of Habeas Corpus; protection for the individual by the state judiciary from actions by judicial officials

anónimos: unsigned mimeographed messages that threatened the lives of Progressive leaders

aprehensiones: office under procurador responsible for arrests

averiguación previa: an investigation made by the ministerio público

cabecera: the district seat

cacique: a political boss

caciquismo: political bossism

calenda: festivities on the first day or first night of a fiesta

campesino: farmer

careo: a formal debate between parties during a district court investigation

cargo: burden or charge

cargo system: village-based system of voluntary service

compadrazgo: ritual co-parenthood

compadre: ritual kin (male)

Conservatives: the Caleros

cuotas: quotas; mandatory contributions by villages to support local projects and fiestas

demanda: complaint

ejecutor: individual employed under the district judge; generally responsible for taking and recording testimony and for keeping court financial and case records

ejido: public land

empleado: employee

escrito: a brief

fonda: small restaurant

ingeniero: engineer

investigaciones: office under procurador and responsible for investigations
investigadores: *See* agente de investigadores
jornaleros: day laborers
juez mixto de primera instancia: district judge
juez tercero: third judge; Oaxaca-based aide in district court investigations
junta: meeting
latifundista: large landowner
lépero: a lowlife; foulmouthed
magistrado: magistrate; judge
mayordoma: lay guardian of the church
mayordomía: sponsorship of a religious fiesta; guardianship of the church
médica legista: individual who reviews autopsy reports for the district judge
mero cacique: top political boss
mesa directiva: a commission chosen to represent a local constituency
mestizo: of mixed races
minifundista: small landowner
ministerio público: the prosecutor for district penal and civil affairs
mozo: porter
municipio: residential unit of 2000 or more inhabitants
municipio libre: semiautonomous political unit that elects its own government
negativos: term used by the Progressives to refer to the Caleros
padre: Catholic priest
palo encerado: tall pine trunk shaved smooth and covered with wax
pedida: a ritualized request for parental permission to marry
perito: individual who assesses physical injuries and property damage and performs autopsies for the local government
petate: woven straw mat
pimienta: black pepper
policía: police
prestaciones: office of loans
primeras diligencias: initial investigation of a dispute; usually conducted by village síndico
principales: elders who have successfully passed through the cargo system and have formed an informal council that establishes policy for elected village officials
proceso: investigation of a case conducted by the district court
procurador general de la república: attorney general
pueblo: town; village
regidor: head of the police force
regidor encargado de las llaves: individual responsible for the district jail and those confined in it
registrar civil: individual who keeps records of births, marriages, and deaths; performs civil marriage ceremonies; and may assist in the preparation of civil documents
rosarios: Catholic recitations
salvo conducta: a formal release from prison
secretários: individuals who share the investigative and administrative duties

of the district judge and the ministerio público when they are present and replace them when they are absent

el seminarista: the padre's assistant; seminarian

síndico: the prosecutor in the village court

sobrecuota: second quota to be paid by all villagers to make up the difference between quotas collected and fiesta costs

subgobernador: assistant to the governor

sucio: dirtied

suplentes: substitutes

tequíos: village work projects

tesorero: individual who collects payments from the village governments for maintenance of persons in jail; the treasurer of the government of the district seat; village treasurer

topil: messenger

torito: sticks bent and covered with paper to resemble a bull's head and covered with firecrackers and sparkler wheels

valiente: brave

viajeros: itinerant merchants

viveros: nurseries

voz pública: the voice of the people; gossip

BIBLIOGRAPHY

Abel, R. 1973. "A Comparative Theory of Dispute Institutions in Society." *Law and Society Review* 8(2): 217–347.

Adams, R. N. 1975. *Energy and Structure: A Theory of Social Power*. Austin: University of Texas Press.

Allot, A. N. 1961. "The Changing Law in Changing Africa." *Sociologus* 11: 115–31.

Anderson, J. N. 1969. "Buy-and-Sell and Economic Personalism—Foundations for Philippine Entrepreneurship." *Asian Survey* 9(9): 641–68.

Anderson, J. N. D. 1963. *Changing Law in Developing Countries*. London: George Allen and Unwin.

Aubert, V. 1963. "Competition and Dissensus: Two Types of Conflict and Conflict Resolution." *Journal of Conflict Resolution* 7(1):26–42.

Bailey, F. G. 1960. *Tribe, Caste, and Nation*. Manchester: Manchester University Press.

———. 1969. *Stratagems and Spoils: A Social Anthropology of Politics*. New York: Schocken Books, Pavilion Series.

Baker, Richard D. 1971. *Judicial Review in Mexico: A Study of the Amparo Suit*. Austin: University of Texas Press.

Barkun, M. 1971. "Law and Social Revolution: Millenarianism and the Legal System." *Law and Society Review* 6(1): 113–41.

Barnes, J. 1968. "Networks and Political Process." In M. Swartz, ed., *Local-Level Politics*, pp. 107–30. Chicago: Aldine.

Barth, F. 1967. "On the Study of Social Change." *American Anthropologist* 69(6): 661–69.

———. 1969. *Ethnic Groups and Boundaries: The Social Organization of Culture Difference*. Boston: Little, Brown.

Barton, R. F. 1919. "Ifugao Law." *University of California Publications in American Archaeology and Ethnology* 15: 1–186.

Beals, R. 1967. "The Structure of the Oaxaca Market System." In *Revista Mexicano de Estudios Antropológicos* 21: 333–42.

———. 1975. *The Peasant Marketing System of Oaxaca, Mexico*. Berkeley: University of California Press.

Bendix, R. 1967. "Tradition and Modernity Reconsidered." In *Comparative Studies in Society and History* 9(3): 292–346.

Benedict, B. 1962. "Stratification in Plural Societies." *American Anthropologist* 64(6): 1235–46.

Bernal, Ignacio. 1958. "Monte Albán and the Zapotecs." *Boletín de Estudios Oaxaqueños* 1 (February): pp. 1–9.

Berry, Charles R. 1981. *The Reform in Oaxaca, 1856–76. A Microhistory of the Liberal Revolution.* Lincoln: University of Nebraska Press.

Bohannon, Paul. 1965. "The Differing Realms of the Law." *American Anthropologist* 67(6), part 2: 33–42.

————. 1980. "You Can't Do Nothing." *American Anthropologist* 82(3): pp. 508–24.

Boissevain, J. 1974. *Friends of Friends.* New York: St. Martin's Press.

Borja Osorno, Guillermo. 1969. *Derecho Procesal Penal.* Puebla, México: Editorial Jose M. Cajica Jr.

Cancian, F. 1965. *Economics and Prestige in a Maya Community: The Religious Cargo System in Zinacantán.* Stanford: Stanford University Press.

————. 1967. "Political and Religious Organization." In Manning Nash and R. Wauchope, eds., *Handbook of Middle American Indians*, vol. 6. Austin: University of Texas Press.

————. 1972. *Change and Uncertainty in a Peasant Economy: The Maya Corn Farmers of Zinacantán.* Stanford: Stanford University Press.

Chance, John K. 1978a. *Race and Class in Colonial Oaxaca.* Stanford: Stanford University Press.

————. 1978b. Indice del Archivo del Juzgado de Villa Alta, Oaxaca: Época Colonial. *Publications in Anthropology No. 21.* Nashville, Tenn.: Vanderbilt University Press.

Cohn, B. S. 1959. "Some Notes on Law and Change in North India." *Economic Development and Cultural Change* 8: 79–93.

Collier, Jane. 1973. *Law and Social Change in Zinacantán.* Stanford: Stanford University Press.

Colson, E. 1953. "Social Control and Vengeance in Plateau Tonga Society." *Africa* 23: 199–212.

————. 1974. *Tradition and Contract. The Problem of Order.* Chicago: Aldine Publishing Company.

Comaroff, J., and S. Roberts. 1977. "The Invocation of Norms in Dispute Settlement: The Tswana Case (1)." In I. Hamnett, ed., *The Social Anthropology of Law.* London: Academic Press.

Coser, Lewis. 1956. *The Functions of Social Conflict.* London: Routledge and Kegan Paul.

Crumrine, Lynne S. 1969. "Ceremonial Exchange as a Mechanism in Tribal Integration among the Mayos of Northwest Mexico." *Anthropological Papers of the University of Arizona Press.*

de la Fuente, J. 1949. *Yalálag. Una Villa Zapoteca Serrana.* Seria Científica I. México City: Museo Nacional de Antropología.

Dennis, Philip A. 1976. *Conflictos por Tierras en el Valle de Oaxaca.* México: Instituto Nacional Indigenista.

Douglas, M. 1970. *Natural Symbols.* New York: Pantheon Books.

Dow, James W. 1974a. *Santos y Sobrevivencia: Funciones de la Religión en Una*

Comunidad Otomí México. México: Instituto Nacional Indigenista, Secretaría de Educación Pública.

———. 1974b. "Public Religion in an Otomí Municipio in the Sierra de Puebla." MS. 1974b.

Epstein, A. L. 1967. "The Case Method in the Field of Law." In A. L. Epstein, ed., *The Craft of Social Anthropology*, pp. 153–80. London: Tavistock.

Evans-Pritchard, E. E. 1940. *The Nuer*. London: Oxford University Press.

Fallers, L. F. 1969. *Law Without Precedent*. Chicago: University of Chicago Press.

Farrell, R. A., and V. A. Swigert. 1978. "Legal Disposition of Inter-Group and Intra-Group Homicides." *Sociological Quarterly* 19(4): pp. 565–76.

Felstiner, W. L. F. 1974. "Influences of Social Organization on Dispute Processing." *Law and Society Review* 9(1): 63–94.

Firth, R. 1954. "Social Organization and Social Change." *Journal of the Royal Anthropological Institute* 84(1): 1–20.

Foster, G. 1967. *Tzintzuntzan: Mexican Peasants in a Changing World*. Boston: Little, Brown.

Frank, Andre Gunder. 1967. *Capitalism and Underdevelopment in Latin America: Historical Studies of Chile and Brazil*. New York: Monthly Review Press.

———. 1972. *Lumpenbourgeoisie, Lumpendevelopment: Dependence, Class, and Politics in Latin America*. New York: Monthly Review Press.

Fuller, L. 1971. "Mediation—Its Forms and Functions." *Southern California Law Review* 44: 305–39.

Garfinkel, Harold. 1956. "Conditions of Successful Degradation Ceremonies." *The American Journal of Sociology* 61(5): 420–24.

Geertz, C. 1963. *Agricultural Involution. The Process of Ecological Change in Indonesia*. Berkeley: University of California Press.

———. 1965. *The Social History of an Indonesia Town*. Cambridge: The MIT Press.

Gibbs, J. L. 1963. "The Kpelle Moot: A Therapeutic Model for the Informal Settlement of Disputes." *Africa* 33: 1–11.

Glacken, C. J. 1967. *Traces on the Rhodian Shore: Nature and Culture in Western Thought from Ancient Times to the End of the Eighteenth Century*. Berkeley: University of California Press.

Gluckman, M. 1955. *The Judicial Process Among the Barotse of Northern Rhodesia*. Manchester: University Press for the Rhodes Livingstone Institute.

———. 1963. "Gossip and Scandal." *Current Anthropology* 4(3): 307–16.

———. 1965. *The Ideas in Barotse Jurisprudence*. New Haven: Yale University Press.

———. 1967. "Introduction." In A. L. Epstein, ed., *The Craft of Social Anthropology*. London: Tavistock.

———. 1969. *Ideas and Procedures in African Customary Law*. M. Gluckman, ed. London: Oxford University Press for the International African Institute.

———. 1973. "Limitations of the Case-Method in the Study of Tribal Law." *Law and Society Review* 7(4): 611–41.

Goody, J. 1975. *Changing Social Structure in Ghana: Essays in the Comparative Sociology of a New State and an Old Tradition*. London: International African Institute.

Graburn, N. H. H. 1969. "Eskimo Law in Light of Self- and Group-Interest."
    Law and Society Review 4(1): 45–60.
Greenberg, James B. 1981. *Santiago's Sword. Chatino Peasant Religion and Eco-
    nomics.* Berkeley: University of California Press.
Gulliver, P. H. 1969. "Introduction." In Laura Nader, ed., *Law in Culture and
    Society,* pp. 11–23. Chicago: Aldine.
————. 1971. *Neighbours and Networks.* Berkeley and Los Angeles: University of
    California Press.
————. 1979. *Disputes and Negotiations. A Cross-Cultural Perspective.* New York:
    Academic Press.
Harris, Marvin. 1964. *Patterns of Race in the Americas.* New York: Walker.
Hine, Virginia. 1977. "The Basic Paradigm of a Future Socio-Cultural System."
    World Issues II(2): 19–22.
Hirabayashi, Lane. 1983. "On the Formation of Migrant Village Associations
    in Mexico: Mixtec and Mountain Zapotec in Mexico City." *Urban Anthropol-
    ogy* 12(1): 29–44.
Hoebel, E. Adamson. 1942. "Fundamental Legal Concepts as Applied to the
    Study of Primitive Law." *Yale Law Journal* 51(6): 951–66.
————. 1954. *The Law of Primitive Man: A Study in Comparative Legal Dynamics.*
    Cambridge: Harvard University Press.
Hunt, E., and R. Hunt. 1969. "The Role of Courts in Rural Mexico." In
    P. Bock, ed., *Peasants in the Modern World.* Albuquerque: University of New
    Mexico Press.
I. F. E. University: Institute of African Studies. 1971. *Integration of Customary
    and Modern Legal Systems in Africa: Papers.* New York: Africana.
Jackson, R. 1977. *Plural Societies and New States: A Conceptual Analysis.* Berkeley:
    Institute of International Studies, University of California.
Johnson, A. J. 1970. *The Organization of Space in Developing Countries.* Cam-
    bridge: Harvard University Press.
Kearney, Michael. 1972. *The Winds of Ixtepeji. World View and Society in a Zapotec
    Town.* New York: Holt, Rinehart and Winston, Inc.
Kelley, Klara Bonsack. 1976. "Dendritic Central Place Systems and the Re-
    gional Organization of Navajo Trading Posts." In Carol Smith, ed., *Regional
    Analysis,* vol. 1, pp. 219–54. New York: Academic Press.
Koch, K.-F. 1974. *War and Peace in Jalemo: The Management of Conflict in High-
    land New Guinea.* Cambridge: Harvard University Press.
Kuper, H., and L. Kuper. 1965. *African Law: Adaptation and Development.*
    Berkeley: University of California Press.
Kuper, L., and M. G. Smith, eds. 1969. *Pluralism in Africa.* Berkeley: University
    of California Press.
Laviada, Iñigol. 1978. *Los Caciques de la Sierra.* México: Editorial Jus.
Leach, E. 1954. *The Political Systems of Highland Burma.* London: Bell.
Lemoine V., Ernesto. 1966. "Algunos Datos Histórico-Geográficos Acera de
    Villa Alta y Su Comarca." In: *Summa Antropológica, En Homenaje a Roberto J.
    Weitlaner,* pp. 193–202. México: Instituto Nacional de Antropología e His-
    toria.

Leslie, C. 1960. *Now We Are Civilized: A Study of the World View of the Zapotec Indians of Mitla, Oaxaca.* Detroit: Wayne State University.

Llewellyn, K. N., and E. A. Hoebel. 1941. *The Cheyenne Way: Conflict and Case Law in Primitive Jurisprudence.* Norman: University of Oklahoma Press.

Malinowski, B. (1926, 1961). *Crime and Custom in Savage Society.* London: Routledge and Kegan Paul.

Mather, L., and B. Yngvesson. 1980–81. "Language, Audience, and the Transformation of Disputes." *Law and Society Review* 15(3–4): 775–821.

Mayer, P. 1961. *Townsmen or Tribesmen: Conservatism and the Process of Urbanization in a South African City.* 2d ed. Cape Town: Oxford University Press, 1971.

Mexico, Leyes y Codigos de. 1969. *Ley Orgánica de Ayuntamientos del Estado Libre y Soberano de Oaxaca.* Oaxaca, México: Publicaciones Loyo Munoz, S. A.

———. 1972. *Codigos de Procedimientos Penales* (Edición 16). México, D.F.: Editorial Porrua, S. A.

———. 1973. *Codigo Civil Para el Distrito y Territorios Federales.* México, D.F.: Editorial Porrua, S. A.

———. 1973. *Codigo de Procedimientos Penales* (Edición 17): México, D.F.: Editorial Porrua, S. A.

———. 1973. *Codigo Penal Para el Distrito y Territorios Federales* (Edición 24). México, D.F.: Editorial Porrua, S. A.

———. 1973. *Codigo Penal y de Procedimientos Penales Para E.L.y S. de Oaxaca.* Puebla, Puebla: Editorial Jose M. Cajica, S. A.

———. 1973. *Ley de Amparo y Ley Orgánica del Poder Judicial de la Federación.* México, D.F.: "Divulgacion."

———. 1974. *Constitución Política de Los Estados Unidos Mexicanos* (Edición 54). México, D.F.: Editorial Porrua, S. A.

———. 1974. *Ley Federal de Reforma Agraria: Exposición de Motivos, Antecedentes, Comentarios y Correlaciones* (Edición 5). México, D.F.: Editorial Porrua, S. A.

Mileski, M. 1971. "Courtroom Encounters: An Observation Study of a Lower Criminal Court." *Law and Society Review* 5(4): 473–538.

Moore, S. F. 1970. "Politics, Procedures, and Norms in Changing Chagga Law." *Africa* 40(4): 321–44.

———. 1973. "Law and Social Change: The Semi-Autonomous Field as an Appropriate Subject of Study." *Law and Society Review* 7: 719–46.

Nader, L. 1964. "Talea and Juquila: A Comparison of Social Organization." *University of California Publications in American Archaeology and Ethnology* 48(3): 195–296.

———. 1965. "Choices in Legal Procedure: Shia Moslem and Mexican Zapotec." *American Anthropologist* 67(2): 394–99.

———. 1966. "Variations in Rincón Zapotec Legal Procedure." In: *Summa Antropológica, En Homenaje a Roberto J. Weitlaner,* pp. 375–83. México: Instituto Nacional de Antropología e Historia.

———. 1969a. "Styles of Court Procedure: To Make the Balance." In L. Nader, ed., *Law in Culture and Society,* pp. 69–91. Chicago: Aldine.

———. 1969b. "The Zapotec of Oaxaca." In Evon Z. Vogt and Robert Wauchope, eds., *Handbook of Middle American Indians*, vol. 7, pp.329–59. Austin: University of Texas Press.

Nader, L., and D. Metzger. 1963. "Conflict Resolution in Two Mexican Communities." *American Anthropologist* 65(3), part 1: 584–92.

Nader, L., and H. Todd, eds. 1978. *The Disputing Process—Law in Ten Societies*. New York: Columbia University Press.

Naroll, R., and W. T. Divale. 1976. "Natural Selection and Cultural Evolution: Warfare versus Peaceful Diffusion." *American Ethnologist* 3:97–128.

Nash, June. 1967. "Death as a Way of Life: The Increasing Resort to Homicide in a Maya Indian Community." *American Anthropologist* 69(5): 455–70.

Nash, Manning. 1958. "Political Relations in Guatemala." *Social and Economic Studies* 7: 65–75.

Orellana S., Carlos L. 1973. "Mixtec Migrants in Mexico City: A Case Study of Urbanization." *Human Organization* 32: 273–83.

Parnell, P. 1978a. "Conflict and Competition in a Mexican Judicial District." Ph.D. dissertation, University of California, Berkeley.

———. 1978b. "Village or State: Competitive Legal Systems in a Mexican Judicial District." In L. Nader and H. Todd, eds., *The Disputing Process—Law in Ten Societies*, pp. 315–50. New York: Columbia University Press.

———. 1982. "Hoebel's Crucible—Information and Misinformation in Case Studies of Law." *Law and Human Behavior* 6(3–4): 379–98.

Parsons, E. C. 1936. *Mitla: Town of the Souls*. Chicago: University of Chicago Press.

Peattie, L. R. 1968. *The View from the Barrio*. Ann Arbor: The University of Michigan Press.

Perez García, Rosendo. 1956. *La Sierra Juárez*, 2 vols. México.

Perez Jimenez, Gustavo. 1955. *La Institución del Municipio Libre en el Estado de Oaxaca y su Reforma Constitucional*. Oaxaca, México: Escuela de Jurisprudencia, Universidad Benito Juárez de Oaxaca.

Pospisil, L. 1967. "Legal Levels and Multiplicity of Legal Systems in Human Societies." *Journal of Conflict Resolution* 11(1): 2–26.

———. 1968. "Kapauku Papuans and Their Law." *Yale University Publications in Anthropology* 54.

———. 1971. *Anthropology of Law: A Comparative Theory*. New York: Harper & Row.

Ravicz, R. S. 1965. *Organización Social de Los Mixes*. México, D.F.: Instituto Nacional Indigenista.

Redfield, R. 1962. *A Village That Chose Progress; Chan Kom Revisited*. Chicago: University of Chicago Press.

Ruffini, J. 1978. "Disputing Over Livestock in Sardinia." In L. Nader and H. Todd, eds., *The Disputing Process—Law in Ten Societies*, pp. 209–46. New York: Columbia University Press.

Sanders, Thomas G. 1986. "Mexico's Emerging Political Crisis." *UFSI Reports*, no. 40 (TGS–13–'85): 1–7.

Selby, H. 1974. *Zapotec Deviance: The Convergence of Folk and Modern Sociology*. Austin: University of Texas Press.

Shibutani, T., and K. M. Kwan. 1965. *Ethnic Stratification: A Comparative Approach.* With contribution by R. H. Billigmeier. New York: Macmillan.

Silverman, S. F. 1965. "Patronage and Community-Nation Relationships in Central Italy." *Ethnology* 4: 172–89.

Smith, Carol, ed. 1976a. *Regional Analysis.* New York: Academic Press.

———. 1976b. "Regional Economic Systems: Linking Geographical Models and Socioeconomic Problems." In Carol Smith, ed., *Regional Analysis,* vol. 1, pp. 1–63. New York: Academic Press.

Smith, Waldemar R. 1977. *The Fiesta System and Economic Change.* New York: Columbia University Press.

Smith, W., and John M. Roberts. 1954. "Zuni Law: A Field of Values." *Papers of the Peabody Museum of American Archaeology and Ethnology,* Harvard University 43(1).

Spradley, J. 1970. *You Owe Yourself a Drunk.* Boston: Little, Brown.

Starr, B. 1954. "Levels of Communal Relations." *American Journal of Sociology* 60(1): 125–35.

Steward, Julian. 1955. *Theory of Culture Change; The Methodology of Multilinear Evolution.* Urbana: University of Illinois Press.

Taylor, W. 1979. *Drinking, Homicide, and Rebellion in Colonial Mexican Villages.* Stanford: Stanford University Press.

Thoden Van Velsen, H. U. E., and W. Van Wetering. 1960. "Residence, Power Groups and Intra-Societal Aggression: An Inquiry into the Conditions Leading to Peacefulness within Non-Stratified Societies." In: *International Archives of Ethnography* 49: 169–200.

Todd, H. F. 1978. "Litigious Marginals: Character and Disputing in a Bavarian Village." In L. Nader and H. Todd, eds., *The Disputing Process—Law in Ten Societies,* pp. 86–121. New York: Columbia University Press.

Turner, V. 1957. *Schism and Continuity in African Society: A Study of Ndembu Village Life.* Manchester: Manchester University Press for the Rhodes Livingstone Institute.

Unger, Roberto. 1976. *Law in Modern Society.* New York: Free Press.

Van Velsen, J. 1967. "The Extended-Case Method and Situational Analysis." In A. L. Epstein, ed., *The Craft of Social Anthropology.* London: Tavistock.

White, L. 1949. *The Science of Culture, A Study of Man and Civilization.* New York: Farrar, Straus.

Whitecotton, Joseph W. 1977. *The Zapotecs: Princes, Priests, and Peasants.* Norman: University of Oklahoma Press.

Witty, C. 1981. *Mediation and Society.* New York: Academic Press.

Wolf, Eric. 1955. "Types of Latin American Peasantry: A Preliminary Discussion." *American Anthropologist* 57(3), part 1: 452–71.

———. 1957. "Closed Corporate Peasant Communities in Mesoamerica and Java." *Southwestern Journal of Anthropology* 13: 1–18.

———. 1967. "Levels of Communal Relations." In M. Nash, vol. ed., *Handbook of Middle American Indians* 6, pp. 299–316. Austin: University of Texas Press.

Yngvesson, Barbara. 1978. "The Atlantic Fishermen." In L. Nader and H. Todd, eds., *The Disputing Process—Law in Ten Societies,* pp. 59–85. New York: Columbia University Press.

INDEX

Adams, Richard: on levels of human relations, 101, 102, 146
Adjudication: and culture conflict, 104; and information, 94, 104; and legitimacy, 104; among Ndendeuli, 92; outcomes of, 107; and simplexties, 107; and social linkages, 99; and social order, 104; and social organization, 108; and stereotypes, 94; in Talean court, 98, 148
Alcadía mayor, 3
Amparo, 48, 134, 143
Analco, 3, 12, 29
Appeal, factors affecting, 15, 89, 90, 147. *See also* Appeals, Oaxacan state system of; Disputes; District court
Appeals, Oaxacan state system of, 14, 125–38; abuse of authority in, 134; access to, 134; *agencia* police, 129; *agente municipal* in, 129–30; *agente de policía* in, 129–30; alcalde in, 88; amparo in, 134; *averiguación previa* in, 127; *careo* in, 128, 131; and *cargo* system, 88, 133; case example of, 134; checks and balances in, 133; correspondence in, 125; criminal investigation in, 125; *de oficio* initiation in, 127; Dirección de Control de Procesos in, 128, 129; district court in, 128; district judge in, 128–32; infractions in, 126; interpreters in, 131; investigations in, 126; judicial police in, 127; *juez del distrito,* 134; and jury trial, 125; *médicas legistas* in, 131; *ministerio público* in, 88, 126–28, 131, 133; *municipio* in, 129; on-site inspections in, 125, 127; patronage in, 127; *peritos* in, 127, 133; police in, 133; procedures in, 88, 125–38; *procuradores general* in, 126; *regidor,* in, 133; reparation of damage in, 127, 134; role of plaintiff in, 125; roles in, 88, 125–38; *síndico procurador* in, 22, 88, 129; and suspension of cases, 131; *tesorero* in, 133; testi-

mony in, 125, 127; training in, 126; and Tribunal Superior del Estado, 88, 130, 131
Arbitration, 62, 107
Autonomy, village, 6, 8; and centralization, 85; in the district seat, 103; in divided villages, 6; history of, 109–10; ethic of, 48; and external forces, 103; and political conflict, 90; and regional assemblies, 83, 84; and social order, 103; and social organization, 56; and the state, 68; and village law, 56; of Zapotec villages, 77

Balance, intergroup relations, role in, 46
Bands: in the district seat, 40, 41; and village divisions, 81
Beals, R., 10
Bernal, Ignacio, 147
Betaza, 51, 81–82, 112, 113
Bohannon, Paul, on segmentary systems, 150
Borja Osorno, Guillermo, 130
Boundaries, village: and external projects, 81; opening of, 80; and political groups, 81; and political parties, 81; and the Protestant church, 106; and regional assemblies, 83; social, of the village, 68
Brokerage, 149; and bureaucracy, 8; and coffee cultivation, 8, 11; effect of Comisión del Compra de Café on, 45; and credit, 7; in the district seat, 7, 16, 45, 65; economic effects of, 140; of information, 16; and intergroup relations, 45; and marketplaces, 8; and political bossism, 40; and political power, 43; and politics of the district seat, 47; and social distance, 149; and stratification, 7; and teachers, 111–12; across villages, 7; in Zapotec villages, 111–12, 140

122–23; and unpredictability, 123; variations in, 122; and the village concept, 85; and the village principle, 104

Lawyers, in village disputes, 79

Leach, Sir Edmund, on relations among political groups, 150

Legal levels: and choice-making, 97; and disputes, 103; escalation of disputes across, 100; and external forces, 103; and legal systems, 97; ordering of, 100; and subgroups, 97

Legal order: and group relations, 96; and legal systems, 96; and social order, 96

Legal privilege, 59

Legal systems: and authority, 100–101; and centralization, 101; disputant evaluation of, 100; of the district seat, 16; and the escalation of disputes, 100; of the extended village, 102; inclusiveness of, 100–101; informal, 15–16; and information, 66, 95, 102; integrative force of, 121; and legal order, 96; and legitimacy, 92; legitimation of, 95; organization of, 95; and organizational principles, 102; and power, 100–101; and regional assemblies, 102; social factors affecting, 101; and social integration, 95; and social order, 96, 121; and social principles, 100; subgroup use of, 101; of subgroups, 96–97; of villages, 15, 102. *See also* Appeals, Oaxacan state system of

Legitimacy: and dispute escalation, 104; of dispute settlement processes, 96; and legal authority, 103; and legal processes, 92; and the narrowing of disputes, 104; of Oaxacan state law, 104; and social order, 104; and social principles, 92

Levels of articulation, 101–2

Levels of integration, 102; in the district seat, 101; and regional assemblies, 84

Levels, social: mediation across, 102; opposition within, 102; ordering of, 102

Market systems: dendritic, characteristics of, 9–10; as mediating mechanisms, 109; Zapotec, 7

Marketplaces: in Camotlán, 8, 10; and centralization, 6; changes in, 10–11; conflicts, over, 43; in the district seat, 3, 8–10, 49; economic roles of, 6; factors affecting the use of, 10; history of 10, 44; in Lachirioag, 8, 10; participation in and coffee cultivation, 140; and

politics, 10; sources of differences across, 10; and stratification, 6; in Yaée, 3, 10; in Yalálag, 3, 10; Zapotec participation in, 111; in Zoogocho, 3, 18

Marriage: and crosscutting ties, 53–56; in the district seat, 53, 55; and group-based conflict, 55; and obligations, 55; and patronage, 54; and political bossism, 54; and political groupings, 53; and social stratification, 54

Mather Lynn: on dispute transformation, 98–99; on the narrowing of disputes, 104

Mayordomía: campesinos, role in, 45; in the district seat, 20, 33, 40, 45, 50, 141, 143; and political conflicts, 66; and political power, 66; and the power of women, 66

Mediation: and compromise, 107; in the district seat, 60; and information, 102; and intergovernmental relations, 65; and legal order, 102; and multiplex ties, 107; across social levels, 102; and social order, 102; and social relationships, 93; and symbolic manipulation, 102; in the Talean court, 148

Mexico City, 56, 79–80; migration to, 4–5; Villaltecos in, 8, 11, 27–28; Zapotec in, 10–11

Middlemen. *See* Brokerage

Migrants: to the district seat, 36, 47, 49, 51, 89; village roles of, 6, 89–90

Migration: and appeal of disputes, 89, 90; from the district seat, 5, 10; in the district seat, impact of, 50, 139; to the district seat, 4, 8, 10, 14, 51, 74; and economy, 9; and kinship, 51; and marriage, 51; to Mexico City, 4; to Oaxaca City, 4; and occupational change, 8; and political bossism, 51; seasonal, 139; and social organization, in the district seat, 51; urban, of Zapotec, 5; from Zapotec villages, 74. *See also* Migrants; Urban migrants

Mines, historical role of, 2, 4, 13–14

Ministerio público, 22–23, 32; and disputes, role in, 61, 75–76. *See also* Appeals, Oaxacan state system of; District court

Mixe: historical roles of, 2, 13; history of, 2; migration to district seat of, 8; and regional assemblies, 83

Moral privilege, 59–60

Morality: and authority, 64; and conflicts, 70; and deviance, 64; and disputes, 69;

ABOUT THE AUTHOR

PHILIP C. PARNELL went to the Philippines for a year in 1987, specifically to Commonwealth, a settlement in metropolitian Manila, to study disputes among the legally landless and homeless and how these disputes shape the futures of the urban poor.

Parnell, a member of the Department of Criminal Justice in the College of Arts and Sciences at Indiana University in Bloomington, received his Ph.D. in anthropology at the University of California at Berkeley and his B.A. in sociology and anthropology at Princeton University.